# SIMPLE SOMATIC THERAPY SOLUTION

30-MINUTE DAILY TRANSFORMATION WITH SOMATIC EXERCISES, VAGUS NERVE STIMULATION, AND HEART RATE VARIABILITY BIOFEEDBACK FOR TRAUMA, ANXIETY, AND DEPRESSION

## HOLISTIC HARMONY PUBLICATIONS

© **Copyright HOLISTIC HARMONY PUBLICATIONS 2025 - All rights reserved.**

The content within this book is copyright-protected. This book is only for personal use. This book may not be reproduced, duplicated, or transmitted in any form or by any means, electronic or mechanical, including photocopying recording, or by any other information storage and retrieval system. You cannot amend, distribute, sell, use, quote, or paraphrase any part of the content within this book without the direct written permission from the author or the publisher.

Under no circumstances will any blame or legal responsibility be held against the publisher or author for any damages, reparation, or monetary loss due to the information contained within this book. Either directly or indirectly. You are responsible for your own choices, actions, and results.

**Legal Notice:**

This book is copyright-protected. This book is only for personal use. You cannot amend, distribute, sell, use, quote, or paraphrase any part of the content within this book without the consent of the author or publisher.

**Disclaimer Notice:**

Please note the information contained within this book is for educational and entertainment purposes only. The information presented in this book is not specific medical advice for any individual and should not substitute medical advice from a health professional. If you have (or think you may have) a medical or psychological problem, speak to your doctor or a health professional immediately about your risk and possible treatments. Do not engage in any care or treatment without consulting a medical professional.

All effort has been expended to present accurate, up-to-date, and reliable, complete information. No warranties of any kind are declared or implied. Readers acknowledge that the author is not engaging in the rendering of legal, financial, medical, or professional advice. The content within this book has been derived from various sources. Please consult a licensed professional before attempting any techniques outlined in this book.

By reading this document, the reader agrees that under no circumstances is the author responsible for any losses, direct or indirect, which are incurred as a result of the use of the information contained within this document, including, but not limited to, — errors, omissions, or inaccuracies.

# CONTENTS

| | |
|---|---|
| *Introduction* | 7 |
| 1. DECODING THE MIND-BODY CONNECTION | 11 |
|    The Science Behind Brain-Body Communication | 12 |
|    Understanding How the Mind Impacts the Body | 17 |
|    How the Body Remembers Past Experiences | 20 |
|    Rewiring the Brain to Heal Trauma | 22 |
| 2. FOUNDATIONS OF SOMATIC THERAPY | 27 |
|    The Foundational History of Somatic Therapy | 28 |
|    The Research-Backed Power of Somatic Healing | 30 |
|    Somatic Therapy Shapes Mind-Body Healing | 32 |
|    From Distress to Calm With Somatic Therapy | 33 |
|    Unveiling Core Techniques of Somatic Therapy | 34 |
|    How Somatic Therapy Unlocks Nonverbal Healing | 36 |
| 3. SOMATIC THERAPY IN UNDER 30 MINUTES | 39 |
|    Daily Grounding for Calm and Emotional Control | 40 |
|    Body Scanning for Awareness and Relaxation | 52 |
|    Progressive Muscle Relaxation to Recharge | 54 |
|    Healing Through Breathing | 57 |
|    Emotions in Motion Fuels Somatic Healing | 61 |
|    Soothing the Senses Support for Mental Health | 68 |
| 4. EMOTIONAL AND PHYSICAL REGULATION THROUGH THE AUTONOMIC NERVOUS SYSTEM | 79 |
|    The Power of the Vagus Nerve | 80 |
|    Fight or Flight Stress Responses | 81 |
|    The Vagus Nerve's Roll in Rest and Recharge | 83 |
|    The Role of Glutamate in Balancing the Brain | 85 |
|    Vagal Tone is the Secret to Emotional Resilience | 86 |
|    The Vagus Nerve Transforms Healing From Trauma | 88 |
|    Improving Vagal Tone for a Balanced Nervous System | 89 |

5. **VAGUS NERVE RESET FOR EMOTIONAL CONTROL AND INNER PEACE** — 93
   - Your Guide to Vagus Nerve Stimulation — 94
   - The Transformative Power of Deep Breathing — 96
   - Build Resilience With Cold Exposure Therapy — 100
   - Humming and Gargling Stimulates the Vagus Nerve — 104
   - Yoga Poses Activate the Vagus Nerve — 109
   - Exploring Vagus Nerve Stimulation (VNS) Devices — 113

6. **HEART RATE VARIABILITY BIOFEEDBACK FOR EMOTIONAL MASTERY** — 115
   - Heart Rate Variability Explained — 116
   - How HRV Reflects Total Physiological Balance — 117
   - Unlocking Wellness With HRV Biofeedback — 119
   - A Step-by-Step Guide to Improving HRV — 121
   - Top Tools for Tracking HRV — 123
   - Interpreting HRV Data for Your Mental Health — 124
   - Powerful Testimonials and Case Studies — 125

7. **THE RHYTHM OF RESILIENCE WITH HRV EXERCISES** — 129
   - Getting Started With HRV Biofeedback — 130
   - Building a Calmer Mind and Body — 131
   - Making HRV Biofeedback Part of Your Routine — 138
   - Studies on HRV for Anxiety and Trauma — 139

8. **BRINGING IT TOGETHER—NEUROSOMATIC THERAPY'S HEALING FORMULA** — 141
   - How NeuroSomatic Therapy Is Harmony at Work — 142
   - Exercises for Anxiety, Stress, and Trauma — 145
   - NeuroSomatic Therapy a New Era in Trauma Care — 151
   - Crafting a Daily Routine for Balance and Well-Being — 158
   - Setting Future Goals for a Path to Healing — 160
   - Overcoming Setbacks and Sustaining Progress — 162

*Conclusion* — 167
*Resources* — 171
*References* — 185

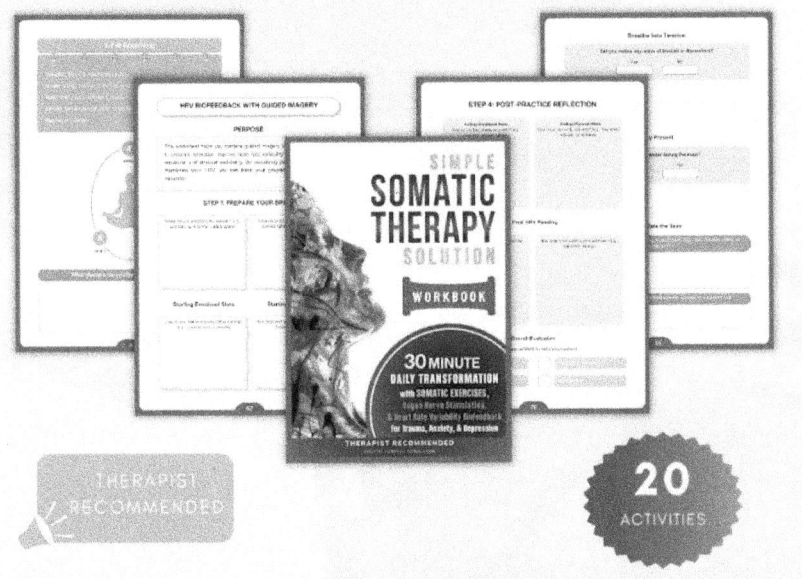

DOWNLOAD YOUR FREE WORKSHEETS NOW!

# INTRODUCTION

> *"It is not the strongest of the species that survive, nor the most intelligent, but the one most responsive to change."*
>
> — CHARLES DARWIN

On a windy, overcast afternoon, Sarah walked into my office, her shoulders heavy with the unspoken burdens she had carried for far too long. Her anxiety and depression had been relentless, refusing to ease despite years of traditional therapy and medication. Each step seemed to echo a sense of isolation, as though she were a stranger in her own body, distanced from the world and herself. Yet, beneath the surface, I sensed a quiet resilience—a desire for relief, genuine connection, and healing. This was where her journey would begin.

We began her journey with somatic therapy, focusing on how her body held on to her trauma. Through gentle, mindful exercises, Sarah started to notice the sensations in her body. She learned to tune into her breath and feel the ground beneath her feet. We introduced vagus nerve exercises to help her calm her nervous system. Gradually, she began to feel more present and less overwhelmed. Integrating Heart Rate Variability (HRV) biofeedback allowed her to see the physical changes in her body as she practiced these techniques. Over time, Sarah's anxiety lessened, and her depressive episodes became less frequent. She found a sense of peace and control she had never known before.

Mental health challenges like trauma, anxiety, and depression are on the rise. Recent studies show that millions of people are affected by these conditions. Traditional therapies often fall short of addressing the complexity of these issues. There is a growing interest in integrative and holistic approaches that consider the mind and body as interconnected.

This book offers a clear, step-by-step guide for mental health practitioners and individuals navigating the challenges of trauma, anxiety, and depression. You'll discover a holistic, evidence-based path to healing through an integrative approach called NeuroSomatic Therapy—combining somatic therapy, vagus nerve stimulation (VNS) exercises, and heart rate variability (HRV) biofeedback. Grounded in scientific research and informed by experts in therapy, psychiatry, and psychology, this method empowers you to address mental health symptoms by targeting the intricate connection between the mind and body.

NeuroSomatic Therapy provides tools to release stored trauma, soothe the nervous system, and gain real-time insights into stress levels. From understanding the profound interplay of your mind and body to mastering practical techniques such as grounding exercises, body scanning, progressive muscle relaxation, and HRV biofeedback, you'll gain the knowledge and skills needed to reclaim emotional and physical balance. The book's structure ensures a seamless learning progression, guiding you from foundational concepts to actionable strategies and real-life applications.

Each chapter builds on the last, introducing powerful methods to regulate stress, improve emotional resilience, and integrate these practices into your daily routine. You'll find actionable insights, practical exercises, worksheets, and daily logs to track your progress and stay motivated. By the end, you'll have a personalized plan for healing and the tools to sustain long-term well-being. With this comprehensive, integrative approach, you'll be equipped to make meaningful strides toward a balanced, resilient life.

I have spent 23 years working in acute treatment settings, helping patients with complex trauma, PTSD, anxiety, and depression. My experience has shown me the transformative power of somatic therapy and integrative techniques. This book is a culmination of my work and research in this field.

This book is for mental health practitioners, adults, men, women, trauma survivors, veterans, and those experiencing anxiety or depression. It addresses their unique challenges and provides practical techniques to implement immediately.

As you read this book, I encourage you to engage with the content actively. Apply the techniques, keep an open mind, and be patient with yourself. Healing is a journey, and these methods can help you find a path to peace and empowerment.

Let us begin this journey together. Healing is possible, and you have the strength to achieve it.

# 1

# DECODING THE MIND-BODY CONNECTION

> "Your body is your subconscious mind. It's trying to tell you what your conscious mind cannot yet understand."
>
> — CANDACE PERT

When John, a war veteran, first came to see me, he was a bundle of nerves and tension. His body seemed to be in a constant state of alert, a remnant of the trauma he had endured.

Traditional therapy had helped him to a degree, but something still felt missing. We began incorporating NeuroSomatic Therapy, focusing on how his body was holding on to the stress and trauma. Through gentle exercises designed to release stored tension and stimulate the vagus nerve, John began to notice subtle but significant changes. His heart rate variability improved, and he started to feel calmer and more in control. This chapter explores the science behind these powerful transformations, showing how the mind and body are intricately connected and how understanding this connection can lead to profound healing.

## THE SCIENCE BEHIND BRAIN-BODY COMMUNICATION

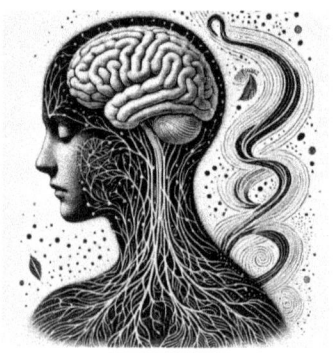

Your brain and body are in constant communication, sending and receiving signals through a complex network of neural pathways. This continuous exchange regulates everything from your heartbeat to your emotional responses. When you experience stress or trauma, these signals can become disrupted, affecting both your physical and emotional well-being.

For instance, when you are stressed, your brain sends signals that trigger the release of stress hormones like cortisol and adrenaline. These hormones prepare your body to respond to a threat by increasing your heart rate, tightening your muscles, and sharpening your focus. While this response can be life-saving in a dangerous situation, chronic stress keeps your body in this heightened state, leading to a range of health problems. By understanding how these signals work, you can use physical interventions to improve your emotional well-being. Techniques like NeuroSomatic Therapy help recalibrate these neural pathways, restoring balance and promoting healing.

*The Role of the Central Nervous System (CNS)*

The central nervous system (CNS), consisting of the brain and spinal cord is the command center for processing sensory information and coordinating responses. It controls both voluntary functions, like moving your arm, and involuntary functions, like breathing. Sensory information from your environment is processed by the CNS, which then decides how to respond. When it comes to emotional regulation, the CNS plays a crucial role.

When you encounter a stressful situation, your CNS processes the threat and mobilizes your body's response. This involves activating specific neural circuits that regulate your emotions. For example, the amygdala, a small almond-shaped structure in the brain, triggers the fight-or-flight response. This response prepares your body to confront or escape the threat. In cases of trauma, these circuits can become overactive, leading to chronic stress and anxiety. By understanding these mechanisms, you can learn how to manage stress more effectively and promote emotional regulation.

*The Function of the Autonomic Nervous System (ANS)*

The autonomic nervous system (ANS) controls many of the body's automatic functions, such as heart rate, digestion, and respiratory rate. It has two main branches: the sympathetic nervous system and the parasympathetic nervous system. The sympathetic system is responsible for the body's fight-or-flight response, preparing you for action in stressful situations. It increases your heart rate, dilates your pupils, and slows digestion to redirect energy to more immediate needs. On the other hand, the parasympathetic system promotes relaxation and recovery, slowing down the heart rate and stimulating digestion.

In trauma recovery, shifting from the sympathetic to the parasympathetic state is crucial. Somatic therapies and vagus nerve exercises facilitate this shift by helping your body recognize and respond to stress signals differently. Techniques like deep breathing, grounding exercises, and mindful movement activate the parasympathetic system, promoting relaxation and healing.

### *Bidirectional Communication via the Vagus Nerve*

The vagus nerve is a critical player in the communication between your brain and body. It connects the brain to major organs, including the heart, lungs, and digestive tract. It plays a vital role in controlling stress and relaxation. When you stimulate the vagus nerve, you activate the parasympathetic system, which helps calm the body and reduce anxiety and trauma symptoms.

Vagus nerve stimulation (VNS) can be achieved through simple exercises like deep breathing, cold exposure, and humming. These practices send signals to your brain to switch from a state of stress to a state of calm, enhancing your ability to manage stress and promoting overall well-being.

**Science-Based Evidence:** Research supports the effectiveness of VNS in promoting relaxation and emotional regulation. A study published in *Frontiers in Psychiatry* demonstrated that deep breathing exercises significantly increase vagal tone, enhancing parasympathetic response and reducing anxiety (Breit, S et al., 2018). Another study published in the *Journal of Health Service Psychology* highlights the potential of vagus nerve stimulation

(VNS) as a non-pharmacological approach for addressing PTSD and related conditions, emphasizing its ability to target excessive sympathetic activity and inflammatory responses, offering a promising therapeutic pathway (Bremner, J. D., 2023).

*Monitoring Heart Rate Variability (HRV) to Improve Mental Health*

Heart rate variability (HRV) measures the balance between stress and relaxation in your nervous system. It reflects how well your body adapts to stress and maintains emotional flexibility. Higher HRV indicates better stress resilience and emotional health, while lower HRV signals stress and poor mental health.

Monitoring HRV biofeedback through wearable devices and phone apps provides real-time data on your body's stress levels, helping you learn to calm your nervous system and manage your emotions more effectively. By monitoring your HRV throughout the day, you can gain insights into your body's stress levels and physical manifestations and use somatic techniques and VNS biofeedback to improve your HRV. Deep breathing, mindfulness, and regular physical activity enhance HRV, helping you manage stress more effectively and improve your emotional well-being.

**Science-Based Evidence:** Research has established a strong link between HRV and mental health. A study published in the *Journal of Affective Disorders* found that individuals with higher HRV exhibited fewer symptoms of anxiety and depression, suggesting that HRV is a reliable marker of emotional resilience (Zhang L. et al., 2023). Additionally, a study in *Frontiers in Psychology* demonstrated that deep breathing exercises and mindfulness practices significantly improve HRV, reducing stress and anxiety (Steffen M. et al., 2021). HRV biofeedback has also been effective; research in the *Journal of Behavioral Medicine* found that regular HRV biofeedback training helped participants achieve a more balanced autonomic nervous system, enhancing their ability to manage stress and improve overall mental health (Lehrer W.E. et al., 2020). These findings reinforce the value of monitoring and improving HRV through targeted psychological and physical well-being practices.

**The Power of Somatic Therapy**

Somatic therapy has gained substantial attention for its ability to help individuals process trauma, anxiety, and depression through body-focused techniques. Research consistently supports its effectiveness in addressing these conditions. Studies show that somatic therapy helps individuals by encouraging them to pay attention to physical sensations and bodily responses. This focus on the body allows people to process unresolved trauma and reduce stress more effectively.

Clinical trials have consistently demonstrated the effectiveness of somatic therapy. For instance, research comparing somatic therapy to traditional talk therapy found that body-based approaches often work better for people with trauma. These studies show significant reductions in PTSD symptoms and improvements in mood. Additionally, people with chronic pain have reported feeling better and moving more freely after regular somatic therapy sessions. Therapists who use somatic therapy with their clients often observe reduced trauma symptoms, enhanced mood, and even improved physical health. This evidence underscores somatic therapy's unique and powerful role in mental health treatment.

**Science-Based Evidence:** A study in the *Journal of Traumatic Stress* found that somatic therapy significantly reduced PTSD symptoms in participants by promoting reconnection with their bodies and facilitating emotional health improvements (Langmuir et al., 2012). Another study comparing somatic therapy to traditional talk therapy revealed that body-based approaches were more effective for trauma recovery, showing marked reductions in PTSD symptoms and mood enhancement (Price, 2005). Research on individuals with chronic pain also supports somatic therapy's benefits; a study in *Philosophy, Ethics, and Humanities in Medicine* reported improvements in movement and pain relief among regular somatic therapy participants (Mehling et al., 2011). These findings emphasize the practical, science-backed benefits of somatic therapy in addressing trauma, anxiety, and chronic pain.

## UNDERSTANDING HOW THE MIND IMPACTS THE BODY

Psychological issues often manifest physically due to the deep interconnectedness of the mind and body. Emotional distress can trigger physiological responses, creating a feedback loop that exacerbates both mental and physical symptoms. Imagine feeling anxious before a big presentation. Your heart races, your palms sweat, and your chest tightens. These are not just figments of your imagination but natural physical responses to emotional stress. Understanding this connection is crucial when addressing conditions like anxiety, depression, and PTSD. By acknowledging that our bodies respond to our emotions, we can use physical interventions to alleviate emotional and physical symptoms, breaking the vicious cycle that keeps us locked in distress.

Anxiety can often lead to chest tightness or shortness of breath. This happens because anxiety activates the body's fight-or-flight response. Even in nonthreatening situations, the sympathetic nervous system kicks in, preparing the body to face or flee from danger. Your heart rate increases and your breathing becomes rapid. This physiological response can make the psychological experience of anxiety even more overwhelming. You may start worrying about the physical symptoms themselves, creating a cycle that feeds on itself. By intervening physically—through deep breathing exercises or grounding techniques—you can calm your body, which in turn helps to calm your mind.

Depression, on the other hand, often manifests as lethargy and a sensation of bodily heaviness. Neurotransmitters like serotonin and dopamine, which play a key role in mood regulation, also affect physical energy levels. When these chemicals are imbalanced, it can lead to feelings of fatigue and heaviness that make daily activities feel like insurmountable tasks. Chronic stress or unresolved emotional issues can exacerbate these symptoms, creating a cycle of emotional and physical exhaustion. Addressing these physical symptoms through somatic techniques can help lift some of this weight, making it easier to tackle the emotional aspects of depression.

When the body encounters a traumatic event, it reacts instinctively to protect itself. Traumatic and stressful events also trigger the same fight-or-flight response. The body gears up to either confront the danger or escape from it. Your heart rate increases, your senses sharpen, and adrenaline surges through your veins. This response is beneficial in immediate danger, preparing you to act swiftly. However, when trauma goes unresolved, this heightened state of alertness can persist. The continuous activation of the fight-or-flight response leads to chronic stress, which in turn can cause physical and emotional problems. Over time, your body might remain in a state of constant vigilance, making it difficult to relax and recover. The nervous system becomes stuck in a perpetual fight-or-flight mode, causing chronic tension that mirrors psychological trauma. Understanding how these physical symptoms are connected to the emotional experience of trauma allows for more effective interventions. Somatic techniques like progressive muscle relaxation and mindful movement can help release this tension, offering relief from both the physical and emotional grip of PTSD.

During traumatic events, the body releases stress hormones like cortisol and adrenaline to keep you alert and ready to respond. While this is essential in the short term, prolonged exposure to these hormones can be harmful. Chronic stress leads to the relentless release of cortisol, which can cause inflammation, lower immunity, and contribute to various health issues. This physical strain often comes with anxiety and depression, creating a challenging cycle that's hard to break. Understanding how these hormones affect your body is critical to developing strategies for managing their impact.

The hypothalamic-pituitary-adrenal (HPA) axis is at the heart of this stress response. It releases cortisol to help you cope with stress. Still, in trauma survivors, it can become overactive, causing problems with emotional regulation and overall well-being. Over time, this chronic activation affects immune function, leaving you more susceptible to illnesses. Recognizing how the HPA axis works underscores why stress management techniques are crucial for both emotional and physical health.

Stress and trauma can also show up physically. Common symptoms include muscle tension, especially in the neck, shoulders, and back, increased heart rate, and palpitations. Chronic tension can lead to headaches, fatigue, and more serious issues like high blood pressure, digestive problems, cancers, and even heart disease. Long-term stress wears down the body's ability to recover, making illness and injury more likely. Emotions often manifest in physical ways: anger might cause clenched fists or a tight jaw, while fear can lead to stomach aches or trouble breathing. Recognizing these physical signs can be a clue to unresolved emotional issues, such as when unexplained pain or digestive issues point to psychosomatic symptoms. Understanding these mind-body connections is vital for developing effective interventions. It highlights the importance of a holistic approach to therapy.

**Science-Based Evidence:** Research in the *Journal of Psychosomatic Research* shows that chronic stress and anxiety activate the sympathetic nervous system and the HPA axis, leading to physiological symptoms like increased heart rate and muscle tension (Thayer et al., 2010). Another study in *Biological Psychiatry* found that patients with depression often have elevated cortisol levels, which contribute to the feeling of physical heaviness (Pariante & Lightman, 2008). These findings underscore the mind-body link and the effectiveness of interventions like deep breathing and progressive muscle relaxation in breaking the psychological and physical distress cycle.

## HOW THE BODY REMEMBERS PAST EXPERIENCES

Our bodies hold on to past experiences, including trauma, in ways that can manifest later as physical or emotional symptoms. These memories are not just stored in the mind but ingrained in our muscles, tissues, and nervous system. This is why someone might experience a sudden tightness in their chest or a

heaviness out of the blue. It is the body's way of recalling past pain, even if the mind has pushed that memory far back. The concept of "body memory" explains why certain physical sensations or movements can trigger emotional responses. For example, a veteran might feel intense anxiety when hearing fireworks, as their body recalls the sounds of gunfire and explosions, even if they are consciously aware that they are safe.

Sensory and somatic memory further illustrate how the body remembers. Sensory memory involves triggers like smells, sounds, or sights that bring back emotional responses. Imagine smelling a specific cologne and suddenly feeling a wave of sadness because it was worn by someone who hurt you. Somatic memory, on the other hand, involves the physical remembrance of trauma. This can manifest as muscle tension, feeling frozen, or other bodily sensations. These memories cause automatic reactions, like muscle tightening or feeling anxious, even if the person does not consciously remember the event. For instance, walking into a building where a traumatic event occurred when you were a child can cause your body to tense up without you realizing why.

Triggers and flashbacks are common in those who have experienced trauma. Triggers are specific stimuli—such as sounds, sights, or physical sensations—that remind the body of past trauma, causing an emotional or physical reaction. For example, the sound of a slamming door might trigger a startle response in someone who has experienced domestic violence. Flashbacks are more intense; there are moments when a person feels as though they are reliving the trauma brought on by a specific trigger, like a smell or sound. It is as if the past invades the present, making the person feel like the traumatic event is happening all over again, even though it is not.

The hippocampus and amygdala play significant roles in how the body holds on to these memories. The hippocampus is responsible for processing and storing memories, but trauma can disrupt its function, leading to fragmented or incomplete memories. This disruption makes it harder for the brain to "file away" trauma properly, leaving these memories unprocessed and easily triggered. The amygdala, which controls fear and anxiety, becomes hyperactive during trauma. This heightened state of alert keeps the body on edge, ready to react. The body holds on to these reactions, making it difficult to relax or feel safe even long after the traumatic event has passed.

Understanding how the body remembers past experiences is crucial for healing. These memories can deeply affect daily reactions, impacting mental and physical health. Recognizing and learning how to address the signs through NeuroSomatic Therapy techniques can help release these stored memories, offering a path to recovery and well-being.

**Science-Based Evidence:** A study in *NeuroImage* demonstrated that trauma can alter the hippocampus and amygdala, leading to heightened sensitivity to triggers (Hayes et al., 2012). Additionally, research in the *Journal of Traumatic Stress* found that somatic therapy significantly reduced PTSD symptoms by helping participants reconnect with their bodies, leading to improved emotional health (Langmuir et al., 2012). These findings highlight the science behind body memory and the potential for somatic interventions to promote healing.

## REWIRING THE BRAIN TO HEAL TRAUMA

Neuroplasticity is a concept that captures the brain's remarkable ability to change and adapt throughout life. Neuroplasticity means our brains can form new connections and reorganize themselves in response to learning, experiences, or healing. This adaptability is especially crucial when recovering from trauma. The brain can forge new pathways years after a traumatic event, allowing for healthier emotional and physical responses. The brain's flexible, dynamic nature offers hope, showing that recovery and improvement are always possible.

The brain's ability to reorganize itself is a cornerstone of mental health and resilience after trauma. When trauma disrupts neural networks, it can lead to maladaptive responses such as chronic stress or anxiety. However, through practices like NeuroSomatic Therapy techniques and mindfulness, we can encourage the brain to rebuild these networks. For example, engaging in deep breathing exercises can help calm the nervous system, creating a new, healthier response to stress. Over time, these practices can help the brain form more robust, resilient pathways. This reorganization is vital to improving mental health, allowing individuals to develop better ways to handle stress and emotional challenges.

New neural pathways are formed through consistent and intentional practices. Imagine walking through a forest. The more you tread the same path, the clearer and more defined it becomes. Similarly, by regularly practicing somatic exercises, you help your brain form new, positive pathways. These practices replace old, trauma-based responses with healthier ones. For instance, mindfulness exercises can help you become more aware of your thoughts and feelings, allowing you to respond rather than react. With time and practice, these new pathways become stronger, making it easier to manage stress and emotions. The brain learns to respond to situations in more balanced and healthy ways.

Neuroplasticity is not just about recovering from trauma but also about enhancing overall mental well-being. You can improve your emotional resilience and adaptability by engaging in activities that promote neuroplasticity. This means that even when faced with challenges, your brain is better equipped to handle them. Techniques like mindful movement, body scanning, and progressive muscle relaxation contribute to this process. These practices help you manage immediate stress and build a foundation for long-term emotional health. The brain's ability to adapt and grow is a powerful tool in the journey toward healing and well-being.

**Science-Based Evidence:** Research in *Nature Reviews Neuroscience* indicates that neuroplasticity plays a significant role in emotional regulation, suggesting that mindfulness and body-focused exercises can lead to lasting changes in brain function (Davidson & McEwen, 2012). Another study in *Psychological Science* found that consistent mindfulness meditation results in structural changes in the brain regions associated with stress and emotional regulation (Hölzel et al., 2011). These findings validate the power of neuroplasticity in healing trauma and improving mental health.

Real-Life Examples: Real-world stories show the benefits of holistic practices. Take Rebecca, who struggled with anxiety and found traditional therapies insufficient. By integrating somatic exercises and monitoring her HRV, she gradually improved her mental and physical health, gaining better control over her emotional responses. Similarly, a veteran managed PTSD symptoms by incorporating mindfulness and body scans into his daily routine, reducing hypervigilance and muscle tension. Another individual with chronic depression found relief through cold therapy, dietary changes, regular exercise, and somatic therapy, which enhanced both mood and quality of life.

Embracing a holistic approach to health requires commitment and consistency, but the rewards—a more balanced, fulfilling life—make the effort worthwhile. By addressing the intricate connection between mind and body, even small changes like practicing mindfulness, engaging in regular movement, or exploring body-focused techniques can create a profound impact. As we move forward, the next chapter will introduce the foundational principles of somatic therapy, offering practical tools to deepen your understanding of this connection and guide you further on your journey to healing and well-being.

## 2

# FOUNDATIONS OF SOMATIC THERAPY

> "When the body speaks, it whispers the truths that the mind fears to utter."
>
> — UNKNOWN

Imagine a veteran named Mike sitting in a therapy room, his hands clenched and his jaw tight. He carries years of trauma in his muscles and bones, feeling disconnected from his body.

Traditional therapy has helped him articulate his fears, but the physical tension remains. When we introduced somatic therapy, Mike learned to pay attention to his body, noticing the tightness in his shoulders and the heaviness in his chest. Through breathwork and gentle movement, he began to release these stored tensions. This approach allowed him to reconnect with his body, offering a path to healing that words alone couldn't provide.

## THE FOUNDATIONAL HISTORY OF SOMATIC THERAPY

Somatic therapy is a holistic approach that bridges the mind and body to help people work through emotional, psychological, and physical distress. Unlike traditional talk therapy, somatic therapy focuses on bodily sensations, using techniques like breathwork, movement, and touch to help process trauma and stress stored in the body. Imagine feeling a knot in your stomach when anxious; somatic therapy enables you to tune into these sensations, understand their origins, and release the tension. Doing so addresses the root of the distress, offering a more comprehensive healing process.

The origins of somatic therapy can be traced back to the early 20th century when pioneers like Wilhelm Reich began exploring the connection between emotional trauma and physical symptoms. Reich, a student of Sigmund Freud, proposed that unresolved emotional issues could manifest as physiological symptoms, such as muscular tension or chronic pain. By releasing these physical manifestations, one could also alleviate the underlying emotional distress. This concept laid the foundation for body-centered psychotherapy, emphasizing that emotions are stored in the body and can be released through physical techniques. In response to traditional psychoanalysis's limitations, this approach introduced techniques like breathwork, movement, and touch to help clients release stored emotions and achieve a sense of balance.

Various therapeutic traditions and insights from trauma research and neuroscience have shaped the evolution of somatic therapy. Reichian therapy emphasized releasing emotional tension through physical methods like breathwork and movement. In contrast, Gestalt therapy, developed by Fritz Perls, contributed to body awareness and experiential techniques. Other bodywork traditions, such as bioenergetic analysis and sensorimotor psychotherapy, further incorporated movement and touch to address emotional and physical imbalances. Research has also shown that trauma can disrupt the brain's normal functioning, leading to changes in behavior and emotional regulation. By addressing these disruptions through somatic techniques, therapists help clients reshape their responses to stress, establishing somatic therapy as a recognized treatment for trauma, anxiety, and depression.

Somatic therapy is rooted in the belief that the body holds on to emotional experiences, and true healing requires addressing these physical sensations. Therapists guide clients to increase awareness of bodily sensations, helping them identify areas of tension or discomfort. Clients can process underlying emotions and release unresolved trauma by focusing on these sensations. Techniques like grounding, movement, and touch facilitate this process, promoting balance and well-being. This evolution has made somatic therapy a widely recognized treatment for trauma, anxiety, and depression. Today, therapists practice it worldwide, offering a powerful tool for healing and emotional well-being.

## THE RESEARCH-BACKED POWER OF SOMATIC HEALING

Research consistently demonstrates the effectiveness of somatic therapy in addressing trauma, anxiety, and depression, with significant benefits for both emotional regulation and physical health. For instance, a randomized controlled trial published in the *Journal of Traumatic Stress* found a substantial reduction in PTSD symptoms among participants receiving somatic therapy compared to those who did not (Langmuir et al., 2012). Similarly, research in the *Journal of Clinical Psychology* highlighted improvements in emotional regulation for patients with chronic anxiety, showcasing the broad applicability of somatic approaches (Bartel et al., 2018).

Neuroscientific evidence further underscores the transformative potential of somatic therapy. Functional MRI (fMRI) studies reveal that somatic practices can alter brain activity patterns associated with trauma and stress, particularly in regions governing emotional regulation and the stress response. By engaging in somatic therapy, individuals can rewire neural pathways, resulting in enhanced emotional stability and a reduction in trauma-related symptoms.

These findings emphasize the importance of integrating scientific research into therapeutic practices. Understanding the specific impacts of somatic techniques allows therapists to create personalized treatment plans tailored to individual needs. For example, evidence showing that particular somatic interventions are highly effective for PTSD enables therapists to incorporate these methods strategically, fostering trust and optimizing outcomes. By grounding therapy in research, practitioners can provide a reliable, client-centered pathway to healing.

Real-life examples from therapists also provide valuable insights into the efficacy of somatic therapy. Consider the case of a military veteran who had struggled with severe PTSD symptoms for years. Traditional therapies offered little relief, but through somatic therapy, he learned to tune into his body's sensations, such as the tightness in his chest and tension in his shoulders, to release the stored trauma. Over time, his flashbacks and hypervigilance diminished, allowing him to regain a sense of control over his emotional responses.

In another example, a young woman named Emily learned to use techniques like breathwork and grounding to manage her severe depression and anxiety, experiencing significant improvement in her overall emotional well-being. These cases highlight somatic therapy's potential to offer a lifeline to those who feel trapped in their own bodies.

In summary, somatic therapy is a powerful, evidence-based approach that addresses both the emotional and physical aspects of mental health issues. The research supports its effectiveness in treating trauma, anxiety, and depression, providing a holistic path to healing. As we move into the following subchapter, we will explore how to integrate these techniques into your daily life for sustained well-being.

## SOMATIC THERAPY SHAPES MIND-BODY HEALING

Somatic therapy rests on foundational ideas emphasizing the deep connection between the mind and body, recognizing that both must be addressed for true healing. At its heart, this approach emphasizes that the key to releasing stored trauma lies in recognizing the inseparable link between emotional and physical sensations. When you experience a stressful event or trauma, it doesn't just affect your mind; it leaves an imprint on your body. Somatic therapy helps you access and release these deep-seated issues by focusing on bodily sensations, facilitating a holistic healing process.

The mind-body connection is central to somatic therapy. It works by raising bodily awareness, helping you identify how your emotions manifest physically, such as tightness in your chest during anxiety or heaviness in your limbs during depression. These physical sensations are not random; they are your body's way of expressing emotional distress. By tuning into these sensations, you can understand the emotional roots of your physical discomfort. This awareness allows you to process and release the trauma stored in your body, breaking the cycle of stress and emotional pain.

Increasing bodily awareness is crucial for identifying and processing underlying emotions. In somatic therapy, you learn to pay attention to physical sensations like tension, discomfort, or pain. This practice involves being present with these sensations and noticing how your body responds to different emotions without judgment. For instance, you might find that the tightness in your shoulders is linked to feelings of fear or anger. By acknowledging and working through these emotions, you can release the physical tension and find relief.

Somatic therapy encourages integrating physical sensations with emotions in a safe, mindful way. You can process emotions without being overwhelmed through guided exercises, such as deep breathing to calm your nervous system or gentle movements to release pent-up energy. Gradually increasing your tolerance for these sensations builds resilience and improves emotional regulation. This integration of body and mind leads to a more effective healing process.

## FROM DISTRESS TO CALM WITH SOMATIC THERAPY

Imagine feeling an overwhelming sense of anxiety that traditional talk therapy has not fully addressed. This is where somatic therapy shines. By focusing on both the physical and emotional aspects of distress, somatic therapy helps individuals release stress and trauma stored in the body. Techniques like breathwork, mindful movement, and body awareness enable access to these deeply rooted issues, facilitating a comprehensive healing process that talk therapy alone may not achieve.

When treating PTSD and complex trauma, somatic therapy provides a safe way to access and release stored memories. For instance, a veteran experiencing flashbacks and chronic tension might notice trauma held in their shoulders or chest. Breathwork helps them stay grounded, allowing these memories to surface and be processed without overwhelming them. This method releases the grip of trauma, reducing symptoms like hypervigilance and emotional numbness and empowering the individual on their recovery journey.

Managing chronic anxiety and depression involves tuning into and regulating physical sensations like tightness in the chest or a racing heart. Somatic therapy teaches you to connect these sensations to your emotions, using techniques like grounding exercises and deep breathing to calm your nervous system. This approach alleviates both the physical symptoms and the overall sense of anxiety. Similarly, for depression, somatic practices ease the sense of heaviness, helping you re-engage with daily life.

Incorporating somatic techniques into your routine promotes emotional regulation and mindfulness, enhancing overall mental well-being. For example, starting your day with a body scan lets you notice tension and consciously relax. This practice fosters a sense of presence and calm, building resilience against stress. Over time, these practices can lead to a more balanced state of mind, helping you navigate life's challenges with greater ease.

## UNVEILING CORE TECHNIQUES OF SOMATIC THERAPY

Somatic therapy offers a variety of techniques that help individuals reconnect with their bodies and release stored trauma. One of the main techniques is grounding exercises. Grounding makes you feel more connected to your body and the present moment, reducing anxiety. These exercises involve focusing on sensory experiences, such as feeling the texture of an object, noticing the weight of your body as you sit or stand, or tuning into the sounds around you. By bringing your attention to these physical sensations, grounding exercises anchor you in the here and now, providing a sense of stability and calm. This can be particularly helpful when you feel overwhelmed or disconnected from your surroundings.

Another key technique in somatic therapy is body scanning. This practice involves mindfully noticing sensations, tension, or discomfort in different body parts. You might start at your toes and slowly work up to your head, paying attention to what you feel in each area. This process helps you  become more aware of how your body holds on to stress and trauma. By identifying these areas of tension, you can begin to release them. Body scanning encourages you to stay present with your physical sensations without judgment, fostering a deeper connection between your mind and body. Over time, this practice can help you release stored trauma and promote overall well-being.

Movement and breathwork are also integral to somatic therapy. Gentle movements, such as stretching or mindful walking, allow emotions to be expressed through the body. Breathwork, which involves deep, intentional breathing exercises, helps regulate the nervous system and create a sense of calm. For instance, diaphragmatic breathing, also known as deep belly breathing, engages the diaphragm and promotes relaxation. As you inhale deeply, your belly rises, and as you exhale, it falls. This type of breathing activates the parasympathetic nervous system, which helps reduce stress and anxiety. Movement combined with breathwork can facilitate the release of emotional tension, helping you feel more balanced and grounded.

These techniques provide a comprehensive toolkit for addressing both the emotional and physical aspects of trauma. Grounding exercises anchor you in the present, body scanning fosters awareness and release of tension, and movement and breathwork promote emotional expression and regulation. Incorporating these practices into your daily routine can improve your emotional resilience and overall mental health. Whether you are a mental health practitioner or someone seeking relief from anxiety and trauma, these techniques offer practical and effective tools for healing.

## HOW SOMATIC THERAPY UNLOCKS NONVERBAL HEALING

In traditional talk therapy, you might spend most of the time discussing your thoughts, feelings, and past experiences. This can be incredibly beneficial but often focuses primarily on verbal expression. Somatic therapy, on the other hand, zeroes in on your bodily sensations and physical responses. Imagine feeling a knot in your stomach when discussing a traumatic event. Somatic therapy encourages you to notice this physical sensation and explore its connection to your emotions. By focusing on how your body feels, somatic therapy helps you access and release stored trauma in ways that words alone cannot achieve. This approach can be remarkably liberating for those struggling to articulate their feelings verbally.

Somatic therapy can seamlessly integrate with other therapeutic methods like Cognitive Behavioral Therapy (CBT), Eye Movement Desensitization and Reprocessing (EMDR), or mindfulness practices. For instance, while CBT helps you challenge and reframe negative thoughts, somatic techniques can help you notice how these thoughts affect your body.

You might combine somatic exercises like grounding or deep breathing with CBT strategies to create a more holistic healing process. Similarly, incorporating somatic methods into EMDR sessions can enhance the processing of traumatic memories by addressing both the emotional and  physical aspects of trauma. This combination allows for a more comprehensive and effective treatment plan.

One of the unique benefits of somatic therapy is its ability to process trauma nonverbally. Many trauma survivors find it difficult to put their experiences into words. Somatic therapy offers an alternative by focusing on physical sensations and movements. For example, you might engage in gentle stretching or mindful movement to express and release stored emotions. This nonverbal approach can be incredibly powerful, allowing you to work through trauma without the need for verbal articulation. It provides a safe and accessible way to process emotions, especially for those who find talking about their trauma overwhelming or retraumatizing.

Somatic therapy also emphasizes self-regulation and empowerment. You learn to manage your emotional and bodily responses through breathwork and grounding exercises. Imagine practicing deep belly breathing when you feel anxious, helping your body shift from a state of stress to relaxation. These self-regulation skills give you the tools to manage your emotions and physical sensations in everyday situations. By empowering you to take control of your healing process, somatic therapy fosters a sense of agency and confidence, enhancing your overall well-being.

Movement and breathwork are integral to somatic therapy, helping you shift out of the fight-or-flight mode that often accompanies trauma. When you engage in mindful movement or deep breathing, you activate the parasympathetic nervous system, which promotes relaxation and recovery. For example, practicing yoga or tai chi can help release physical tension and calm your mind. These practices create a sense of balance and peace, allowing your body to recover from the effects of trauma. Movement and breathwork are natural and effective ways to support your healing process.

Somatic therapy leverages the body's natural healing mechanisms, such as neuroplasticity, to reset the nervous system and recover from trauma. Neuroplasticity is the brain's ability to reorganize and form new neural connections. Engaging in somatic practices helps your brain create healthier pathways for responding to stress and emotions. Techniques like body scanning and progressive muscle relaxation (PMR) encourage this rewiring process, promoting emotional and physical resilience. This natural healing approach aligns with the body's inherent capacity for recovery, offering a holistic and sustainable path to well-being.

As we have explored in this chapter, somatic therapy offers a holistic approach to healing by addressing the body and mind as a unified whole. The science, principles, and techniques of somatic therapy reveal its profound impact on mental and physical health, providing tools for individuals to access and release deep-seated trauma.

# 3

# SOMATIC THERAPY IN UNDER 30 MINUTES

> "Every moment of your life is encoded in your body. Healing is the process of bringing awareness to the story it tells."
>
> — DEB SHAPIRO

Imagine standing in a crowded room, your heart pounding, your breath shallow, and your mind racing. This is what anxiety and trauma can feel like—overwhelming and inescapable. For many, somatic therapy offers a lifeline, a way to anchor themselves in the present moment and regain a sense of control. Somatic therapy focuses on engaging the body and nervous system directly to stabilize emotions and manage the immediate symptoms of anxiety, depression, and trauma. These techniques are particularly essential for trauma survivors, as they help bring attention back to the body and the present moment, providing relief from dissociation and panic attacks.

Remember to grab your free bonus worksheets by SCANNING THE BARCODE BELOW! These tools are designed to enhance the exercises in this chapter and guide you on your healing journey.

DAILY GROUNDING FOR CALM AND EMOTIONAL CONTROL

Grounding techniques work differently from traditional therapies by focusing on the physiological level. While talk therapy addresses the cognitive and emotional aspects, grounding techniques engage the body and nervous system to promote immediate relief. Imagine feeling a wave of anxiety coming on; instead of getting caught in a spiral of negative thoughts, grounding techniques help you focus on the here and now. By doing so, they interrupt the cycle of anxiety and provide a tangible way to manage symptoms. These simple yet powerful methods offer immediate and long-term emotional regulation and healing benefits.

### The 5-4-3-2-1 Technique

**Purpose:** The 5-4-3-2-1 technique is one of several grounding methods that can be particularly effective, as it engages the senses to bring you back to the present moment. You start by listing five things you can see, four things you can touch, three things you can hear, two things you can smell, and one thing you can taste. This sensory engagement helps distract your mind from anxious thoughts and focuses your attention on your surroundings. Over time, practicing this technique can enhance your ability to stay present and emotionally regulated.

1. **Find a comfortable position.** Sit or stand in a relaxed position and take a deep breath to begin.
2. **Name five things you can see.** Look around and slowly name five things you can see. Say them out loud or in your mind, focusing on the details.
3. **Identify four things you can touch.** Notice four things you can physically touch around you. Feel their textures and sensations with your hands.
4. **Listen for three sounds.** Close your eyes if comfortable and listen. Identify three sounds you can hear, whether they're loud, soft, close, or far away.
5. **Notice two things you can smell.** Take a deep breath and identify two distinct smells. If nothing stands out,

focus on the air you breathe in or use a scented item like lotion.
6. **Recognize one thing you can taste.** Pay attention to your mouth and identify one taste. If needed, take a sip of water or chew gum to help with this step.
7. **Repeat as needed.** Continue this process until you feel calmer and more grounded in the present moment.

*Deep Belly Breathing Technique*

**Purpose:** Deep belly breathing, also known as diaphragmatic breathing, is another effective grounding technique. This method involves breathing deeply into your diaphragm, which activates the parasympathetic nervous system and promotes relaxation. When you breathe deeply, you send a signal to your brain that it's safe to relax, reducing anxiety and stress. This technique provides immediate calming effects and, with regular practice, helps manage stress and trauma over the long term.

1. **Find a comfortable position.** Sit or lie down in a relaxed position, placing one hand on your chest and the other on your abdomen.
2. **Inhale slowly.** Breathe in deeply through your nose for a count of four. Focus on expanding your abdomen as you inhale rather than your chest. You should feel the hand on your abdomen rise while the hand on your chest remains still.
3. **Hold your breath.** Gently hold your breath for a count of two to let the air settle into your diaphragm.
4. **Exhale slowly.** Breathe out through your mouth for a count of six, feeling your abdomen fall as you release the air. Make a soft "whoosh" sound as you exhale to enhance the relaxation effect.

5. **Repeat** this process for 5–10 breaths or until you feel more relaxed and grounded. Practice regularly to strengthen your body's relaxation response.

*Physical Grounding Techniques*

**Purpose:** Physical grounding techniques, such as touching a textured object, stomping your feet, or walking barefoot in nature, can be highly effective in reconnecting you with your body and the physical world. These methods provide immediate relief from anxiety and promote long-term emotional stability. For example, holding a grounding object, like a stress ball, and focusing on its texture can help anchor you in the present moment. Similarly, pressing your feet firmly into the ground can enhance your sense of connection. Over time, these techniques can improve your ability to regulate emotions and stay grounded during stressful situations.

1. **Choose a grounding object.** Find a small object with a distinct texture, such as a stress ball, stone, or fabric. Keep it nearby for easy access when you feel anxious.
2. **Focus on texture.** Hold the object in your hand and focus on its texture. Notice its temperature, weight, and how it feels in your palm. Move your fingers over its surface and pay attention to every sensation.
3. **Press your feet into the ground.** Press your feet firmly into the ground while sitting or standing. Feel the connection between your feet and the surface beneath you. Wiggle your toes and notice how the ground supports you.
4. **Engage your senses.** If possible, walk barefoot on a natural surface like grass or sand. Feel the textures and temperatures as you walk, focusing on each step.

5. **Breathe and notice.** Take slow, deep breaths while focusing on the sensations in your hands or feet. This will help you stay present and enhance the grounding effect.
6. **Repeat as needed.** Use these physical grounding techniques whenever you feel overwhelmed. With regular practice, they can become a reliable tool for managing stress and anxiety.

*Mental Grounding Techniques*

**Purpose:** Mental grounding techniques, such as counting backward from 100, can effectively shift your focus away from anxiety or panic. This mentally engaging activity provides immediate relief by distracting you from distressing thoughts and emotions. Over time, practicing this technique can enhance your ability to manage anxiety and racing thoughts more effectively.

1. **Find a quiet space.** Sit or stand in a comfortable, quiet space where you can focus without interruptions.
2. **Take a deep breath.** Before you begin, take a slow, deep breath to help center yourself.
3. **Start counting.** Slowly start counting backward from 100. Say each number out loud or in your mind, focusing your attention on each one as you go.
4. **Visualize each number.** As you count, try to picture each number in your mind. This added mental imagery can help further distract you from anxious thoughts.
5. **Slow down if needed.** If you find your mind wandering back to anxiety, slow down your counting. You can even pause between numbers to deepen the calming effect.
6. **Repeat as needed.** Continue counting backward until you notice decreased anxiety. You can repeat this exercise

whenever you feel overwhelmed to help manage distressing thoughts.

*Sensory Grounding Techniques*

**Purpose:** Sensory grounding techniques, such as aromatherapy, listening to calming music, or focusing on the sounds around you, can quickly reduce anxiety symptoms and help you reconnect with the present moment. Engaging your senses in this way provides immediate relief and promotes long-term emotional healing. For instance, calming music can soothe your mind and body, offering a break from anxious thoughts.

1. **Choose a sense to focus on.** Decide whether you want to engage your sense of smell, sound, or touch. You can also combine multiple senses if that feels helpful.
2. **Use aromatherapy.** If using aromatherapy, select a calming scent such as lavender, eucalyptus, or chamomile. Place a drop of essential oil on a cotton ball or use a diffuser. Take slow, deep breaths, focusing on the scent as you inhale.
3. **Listen to calming music.** Find a piece of calming music or nature sounds. Close your eyes and focus on the rhythm, melody, or individual instruments. Let the sound wash over you, pulling your attention away from anxious thoughts.
4. **Tune into surrounding sounds.** If using the sounds around you, close your eyes and take a moment to listen. Identify and focus on different sounds, like birds chirping, distant conversations, or the hum of a fan.
5. **Notice physical sensations.** If you are engaging in touch, grab a soft or textured item, like a blanket or stress ball.

Focus on how it feels against your skin, noticing every detail.
6. **Repeat as needed.** Continue the sensory grounding for as long as needed. Practice regularly to enhance your ability to manage anxiety and improve your overall emotional resilience. Over time, you will find these techniques more accessible, allowing you to ground yourself more quickly in challenging situations.

*Walking Grounding*

**Purpose:** Walking grounding involves slow, intentional movement to reconnect with your body and environment. This technique provides immediate relief from restlessness or anxiety and promotes long-term presence and emotional regulation. By focusing on the physical sensations of walking, you can anchor yourself in the present moment and reduce anxiety.

1. **Find a safe space.** Choose a quiet, safe area where you can walk uninterrupted, either indoors or outdoors.
2. **Start slowly.** Begin walking at a slow, comfortable pace. Let your arms hang naturally at your sides, and focus on each step.
3. **Focus on sensations.** Pay close attention to the physical sensations as you walk. Notice how your feet make contact with the ground, how your legs move, and how your body shifts with each step.
4. **Engage your senses.** As you walk, observe your surroundings. Notice what you see, hear, and smell. Feel the texture of the ground beneath your feet, whether it's grass, pavement, or carpet.
5. **Sync with your breath.** Take deep, slow breaths as you walk. Inhale through your nose, feel the air fill your lungs,

and exhale through your mouth, syncing your breathing with your steps.
6. **Repeat as needed.** Continue this mindful walking for several minutes or until you feel more grounded. Use this technique whenever you need to reconnect with your body and the present moment.

*Temperature Changes*

**Purpose:** Temperature changes can also be an effective grounding method, such as holding cold or warm objects. Sudden temperature shifts can refocus your attention away from distressing emotions and provide immediate relief. For example, holding an ice cube in your hand can bring your focus to the cold sensation, distracting you from anxious thoughts.

1. **Choose your object.** Select a temperature-based object to use, such as an ice cube, a cold drink, a warm mug, or a heating pad.
2. **Hold the object.** Place the chosen object in your hand. If using an ice cube, hold it in your palm and let the cold sensation spread. If using a warm object, feel the heat radiating through your hand.
3. **Focus on the sensation.** Direct your full attention to the sensation of the cold or warmth. Notice how your skin reacts to the temperature and how it feels against your hand.
4. **Take deep breaths.** Take slow, deep breaths while holding the object. Inhale through your nose, feeling the cool or warm air, and exhale through your mouth.
5. **Engage other senses.** If helpful, describe the sensation to yourself. For example, say, "I feel the coldness spreading across my palm," or "The warmth is soothing and relaxing."

6. **Repeat as needed.** Continue holding the object until you feel more grounded. Use this technique whenever you need a quick distraction from anxiety or distressing emotions.

*Creative Grounding Methods*

**Purpose:** Creative grounding methods, such as drawing, painting, diamond art painting, or journaling, can also be highly effective. Engaging in creative activities helps focus your mind and express emotions, offering immediate relief from anxiety or trauma-related symptoms. These activities also promote long-term emotional regulation and healing, fostering mindfulness and a deeper connection to the present moment.

1. **Choose your activity.** Select a creative activity that appeals to you, such as drawing, painting, diamond art, or journaling. Keep your supplies easily accessible for when you need them.
2. **Set up your space.** Find a quiet, comfortable place to focus on your chosen activity. Arrange your supplies in front of you, taking a moment to appreciate the colors, textures, or tools you'll be using.
3. **Begin slowly.** Start your creative process slowly. If you're drawing or painting, begin with simple strokes or shapes. For journaling, start by writing down whatever comes to mind without judgment. If using diamond art, focus on placing one gem at a time.
4. **Engage your senses.** Pay close attention to the sensations involved in your activity. Notice the feel of the pen or brush in your hand, the sound of the pencil on the paper, or the texture of the gems.

5. **Express your feelings.** Use this time to express your emotions through your art or writing. Let your thoughts and feelings flow onto the paper or canvas, allowing the process to help you release tension.

6. **Focus on the present.** Keep your mind focused on the task at hand. If your thoughts drift, gently bring your attention back to the activity.
7. **Repeat as needed.** Continue the creative grounding until you feel more relaxed and centered. Use this technique whenever you need to reconnect with yourself and the present moment.

*Personalized Grounding Techniques*

**Purpose:** Personalized grounding techniques can be tailored to suit individual needs, trauma histories, or specific triggers. For trauma survivors, veterans, and individuals with chronic anxiety, it's important to customize these techniques to ensure they are safe and effective. For example, a trauma survivor might find relief in physical grounding during a panic attack. At the same time, a veteran might use mental grounding techniques to manage flashbacks. Adapting these techniques based on personal experiences ensures they provide the most benefit.

1. **Identify your needs.** Take a moment to reflect on your specific triggers and the symptoms you experience, such as anxiety, flashbacks, or panic attacks. Understanding your unique situation will help you choose the most effective grounding techniques.
2. **Experiment with different methods.** Try various grounding techniques, such as physical (e.g., holding an object), mental (e.g., counting backward), or sensory (e.g., listening to calming music). Pay attention to how each method makes you feel.

3. **Assess what works.** After trying different techniques, note which ones provide the most immediate relief and sense of calm. Consider when and how each technique is most effective, such as during moments of anxiety or flashbacks.
4. **Create a grounding plan.** Create a personalized grounding plan based on what works best for you. Include specific techniques you find helpful and decide when to use each one. For example, use physical grounding during panic attacks or mental grounding for racing thoughts.
5. **Practice regularly.** Incorporate your chosen techniques into your daily routine, even when you are not experiencing distress. Regular practice helps strengthen your ability to use these methods effectively during stressful situations.
6. **Adjust as needed.** Over time, reassess your grounding plan. Modify your techniques as your needs change, ensuring they remain effective and supportive of your emotional well-being.

Consider the case of an individual with social anxiety who uses sensory grounding techniques to manage their anxiety in social settings. By focusing on the texture of a small object in their pocket, they can distract themselves from anxious thoughts and stay present. Similarly, a trauma survivor might employ physical grounding during a panic attack, such as stomping their feet or holding on to a textured object, to find immediate relief. A veteran might use mental grounding techniques, like counting backward from 100, to manage flashbacks and regain control during moments of distress. These examples highlight the practical impact of grounding techniques and their effectiveness in managing anxiety and trauma symptoms.

## BODY SCANNING FOR AWARENESS AND RELAXATION

### Body Scan Meditation: A Path to Relaxation and Resilience

Body scan meditation is a mindfulness practice that promotes relaxation, enhances body awareness, and helps you reconnect with the present moment. Focusing on different parts of your body and noticing sensations, tension, or discomfort allows you to release physical stress and deepen the mind-body connection. It offers insight into how your body retains stress and trauma, fostering immediate relaxation and contributing to long-term emotional regulation.

Regular practice of body scanning goes beyond relaxation, building self-awareness and emotional insight. By tuning into your body consistently, you can identify stress responses early and take proactive steps to manage them. Over time, this heightened awareness enhances your ability to handle anxiety and tension, promoting better mental and physical well-being.

The science of body scanning highlights its profound effects on the nervous system. This practice activates the parasympathetic nervous system, shifting your body from a fight-or-flight state to one of rest and recovery. This reduces stress hormones like cortisol and trains your nervous system to respond more effectively to stress, increasing resilience and emotional balance. Incorporating body scanning into your routine can create lasting improvements in your overall well-being.

*Body Scanning*

1. **Find a comfortable position.** Sit or lie down in a quiet space where you won't be disturbed. Close your eyes and take a few deep breaths to center yourself.
2. **Start at the top of your head.** Begin by bringing your attention to the top of your head. Notice any sensations—discomfort, tightness, warmth, or tingling, for example, tightness in your forehead or heaviness in your chest; stay present with these sensations—without judgment. Observe what you feel.
3. **Move down your body.** Slowly move your attention downward, focusing on different parts of your body one at a time—your forehead, face, neck, shoulders, arms, chest, stomach, hips, legs, and feet. Take your time with each area, noticing how each part feels, and allow yourself to relax deeper.
4. **Breathe into tension.** If you encounter areas of tension or discomfort, take a deep breath and imagine sending your breath to that area. As you exhale, visualize releasing any tension from your body.
5. **Stay present.** If your mind starts to wander, gently bring your focus back to the sensations in your body. Remember, this exercise is about noticing, not fixing or analyzing.
6. **Complete the scan.** Once you've scanned your entire body, take a moment to notice how you feel overall. You may feel more relaxed, aware, or connected to your body.
7. **Repeat as needed.** Practice this body scan daily or whenever you feel disconnected from your body. Regular use of this technique can enhance your ability to manage stress and anxiety.

Body scanning can be adapted to suit individual needs, offering flexibility in practice. A 5-minute body scan can provide rapid relaxation and increased bodily awareness for a quick daily routine. This shorter version focuses on key areas of tension, allowing you to identify and release stress quickly. For deeper relaxation, an extended 30-minute body scan offers a more thorough exploration of bodily sensations. This extended practice allows you to spend more time on each body part, promoting a deeper sense of relaxation and connection. By tailoring the practice to your needs, you can ensure that body scanning remains an effective tool for your mental and physical health.

## PROGRESSIVE MUSCLE RELAXATION TO RECHARGE

Progressive Muscle Relaxation (PMR) is a mindfulness technique that systematically tenses and relaxes muscle groups to relieve physical tension and reduce anxiety. Developed by Dr. Edmund Jacobson in the early 20th century, PMR is based on the principle that physical relaxation can help alleviate psychological stress. By focusing on the sensations of tension and release in each muscle group, this practice provides immediate stress relief and long-term benefits for managing trauma, anxiety, and tension.

Practicing PMR helps increase body awareness, allowing you to recognize and release stress-related tension. The process signals to the brain that it's safe to relax, reducing the intensity of anxious thoughts and feelings. Regular practice of PMR has been shown to improve sleep quality, enhance emotional regulation, and promote a sense of calm.

To maximize its effectiveness, practice PMR in a quiet, comfortable space. Performing PMR before bed can improve sleep, and using it during stressful moments provides immediate relief. Consistent practice makes it easier to relax and manage stress over time, supporting long-term mental and physical health.

For example, Matt, who struggled with chronic stress, found that 20 minutes of PMR each evening reduced his stress levels and helped him regain emotional control. Similarly, Katie, who battled anxiety and insomnia, experienced better sleep and reduced anxiety through regular PMR sessions. These stories highlight the transformative potential of PMR in fostering resilience and well-being.

*Progressive Muscle Relaxation (PMR)*

1. **Find a quiet, comfortable space.** Find a quiet place where you won't be disturbed for your PMR session. Sit or lie down in a relaxed position.
2. **Center yourself with deep breaths.** Take a few slow, deep breaths to center yourself and focus your mind. Inhale through your nose for a count of four, hold for two, and exhale through your mouth for a count of six.
3. **Start with your feet.** Begin with your feet. Tense the muscles in your toes for 5–10 seconds, then slowly release the tension. Focus on the sensation of relaxation that follows.

4. **Work your way up.** Gradually move up your body, focusing on one muscle group at a time. Tense and relax the following areas:
   - Calves
   - Thighs
   - Abdomen
   - Chest
   - Hands
   - Arms
   - Shoulders
   - Neck
   - Face and Head
5. **As you tense each muscle group, hold the tension for 5–10 seconds before releasing.** Pay close attention to the contrast between the tension and the relaxation.
6. **Focus on sensations of relaxation.** After releasing tension from each muscle group, concentrate on the feeling of relaxation. Notice how the muscles soften and the stress dissipates from your body.
7. **Adjust for shorter sessions.** A quick 5–10-minute PMR session can relieve immediate stress if you're short on time. Focus on key areas of tension, such as your shoulders, neck, and jaw. Use the same tensing and relaxing technique to achieve a quick but effective release.
8. **Repeat as needed.** Practice PMR regularly to improve your ability to manage tension and stress. You can perform an entire 30-minute session when time permits or use a shorter version for quick relief during moments of anxiety.

## HEALING THROUGH BREATHING

Breathing is something we all do unconsciously, yet it becomes a transformative tool for healing when practiced intentionally. In somatic therapy, breathing exercises are not just about inhaling and exhaling—they are powerful techniques for calming the nervous system, managing stress, and promoting emotional healing. Whether you are navigating anxiety, trauma, or chronic stress, integrating specific breathing practices into your routine can profoundly impact your mental and physical well-being.

The science is clear: Controlled breathing activates the parasympathetic nervous system, shifting the body from a fight-or-flight state to one of rest and recovery. Techniques like diaphragmatic, box, and alternate nostril breathing lower stress hormones, reduce anxiety, and enhance emotional regulation. Studies have demonstrated that these practices directly influence the brain, fostering balance and relaxation while reducing symptoms of PTSD, anxiety, and depression.

The benefits extend beyond the mind. Physically, intentional breathing increases oxygen flow, relieves muscle tension, and promotes relaxation. It helps release pent-up energy stored in the body, an essential part of trauma recovery in somatic therapy. Many individuals, like Janette and James, have experienced life-changing effects from breathing techniques, finding relief from panic attacks, hypervigilance, and sleep issues.

Breathing exercises are accessible, easy to practice, and offer immediate relief and long-term benefits. In the next section, you will explore techniques designed to support your emotional and physical healing, helping you reconnect with your body, regulate emotions, and build resilience. Let your breath be the foundation for restoring balance and finding peace.

### *Diaphragmatic Breathing (Deep Belly Breathing)*

**Purpose:** Diaphragmatic breathing, also known as deep belly breathing, engages the diaphragm and encourages full oxygen exchange, helping to calm the nervous system and reduce stress.

1. **Find a comfortable position.** Sit or lie down in a comfortable position with your hands resting on your abdomen.
2. **Take a deep breath in.** Slowly inhale through your nose for a count of four. Focus on expanding your diaphragm—your stomach should rise, but your chest should remain still.
3. **Hold the breath.** Hold the breath for a count of two, allowing the oxygen to circulate.
4. **Exhale slowly.** Exhale slowly through your mouth for a count of six. Feel your abdomen gently fall as the air leaves your body.
5. **Repeat** this process for 5–10 breaths or until you feel more relaxed and centered.

### *Box Breathing (4-4-4-4 Method)*

**Purpose:** Box breathing is a structured breathing technique that helps calm the mind and body by promoting mindfulness and slowing the breath.

1. **Find a quiet space.** Sit or stand in a quiet, comfortable place where you won't be interrupted.
2. **Inhale for four counts.** Inhale slowly through your nose for a count of four, focusing on filling your lungs completely.
3. **Hold for four counts.** Hold your breath for another four counts, feeling the stillness.
4. **Exhale for four counts.** Slowly exhale through your mouth for four counts, emptying your lungs.
5. **Hold for four counts again.** Hold your breath again for a final count of four before starting the next cycle.
6. **Repeat.** Continue this process for at least five cycles or until you feel a sense of calm.

### *4-7-8 Breathing*

**Purpose:** 4-7-8 Breathing helps calm the mind and body by using extended exhales to promote deep relaxation.

1. **Get comfortable.** Sit or lie down in a comfortable position with your hands resting on your abdomen.
2. **Inhale for four counts.** Breathe in slowly through your nose for a count of four, filling your lungs completely.
3. **Hold for seven counts.** Hold your breath for a count of seven, keeping your body relaxed.
4. **Exhale for eight counts.** Slowly exhale through your mouth for a count of eight, letting go of all the air in your lungs.
5. **Repeat.** Continue this pattern for 4–5 cycles or until you feel more relaxed.

### *Alternate Nostril Breathing*

**Purpose:** Alternate nostril breathing helps balance the nervous system and reduce stress by alternating breath through each nostril.

1. **Find a relaxed position.** Sit comfortably with your spine straight.
2. **Close your right nostril.** Use your right thumb to close off your right nostril.
3. **Inhale through the left nostril.** Slowly inhale through your left nostril for a count of four.
4. **Switch nostrils.** Close your left nostril with your right ring finger and release your right nostril.
5. **Exhale through the right nostril.** Exhale through the right nostril for a count of four.
6. **Inhale through the right nostril.** Inhale through your right nostril for a count of four, then switch again, closing the right nostril and opening the left.
7. **Exhale through the left nostril.** Exhale through your left nostril for a count of four.
8. **Repeat.** Continue alternating nostrils for 5–10 cycles.

### *Pursed Lip Breathing*

**Purpose:** Pursed lip breathing helps slow your breathing rate, easing tension and stress.

1. **Sit in a comfortable position.** Relax your shoulders and neck and sit in a comfortable position.
2. **Inhale through your nose.** Inhale through your nose for two counts, keeping your mouth closed.

3. **Purse your lips.** Pucker your lips like you're about to whistle.
4. **Exhale slowly.** Exhale slowly through your pursed lips for a count of four, letting out all the air in your lungs.
5. **Repeat.** Continue this process for 5–10 breaths or until you feel a stress reduction.

Regular breathwork offers numerous benefits, including improved emotional regulation, reduced stress, and better sleep quality. By incorporating breathing exercises into your daily routine, you can enhance your ability to manage stress and anxiety effectively. Set reminders for regular practice to establish a habit, and consider practicing breathwork in the morning to start your day calmly. Use breathing exercises during stressful moments for immediate relief and combine breathwork with other somatic exercises for enhanced emotional regulation.

## EMOTIONS IN MOTION FUELS SOMATIC HEALING

Movement is a vital component of somatic therapy, offering a way to alleviate symptoms of trauma, anxiety, and depression. It releases endorphins, natural mood elevators that reduce stress and enhance well-being. Movement also allows for emotional expression, helping you process and release stored emotions, creating a bridge between your physical and emotional selves.

Techniques like gentle yoga, tai chi, and freeform dance are integral to somatic therapy. Yoga poses such as Child's Pose or Cat-Cow promote relaxation and grounding, while tai chi's slow, mindful movements enhance focus and reduce stress. Dance offers a liberating method of self-expression, enabling intuitive movement that helps process emotions and reconnect with your body.

Stories like Lisa, who overcame trauma through dance therapy, and Samuel, who found emotional balance with yoga, showcase the transformative power of movement. These practices foster healing, helping you release tension, regain balance, and reconnect with yourself.

***Calm Within: Gentle Yoga Poses for Emotional Harmony***

**Purpose:** Gentle yoga poses are a powerful tool to release physical tension and promote emotional balance. These simple poses, such as **Child's Pose** and **Cat-Cow**, help you connect with your body and calm your mind. Regularly practicing these poses can help you reduce stress, enhance mindfulness, and restore balance to your nervous system.

1. **Find a quiet, comfortable space.** Find a comfortable space to practice undisturbed. Use a yoga mat or a soft surface to support your knees and hands.
2. **Start with Child's Pose (Balasana).**
    - **Kneel on the floor.** Kneel down, bringing your big toes together and sitting back on your heels.
    - **Extend your arms.** Stretch your arms forward, palms facing the mat, and slowly lower your forehead to the ground.
    - **Relax into the pose.** Let your shoulders relax, and your chest melts toward the floor. Breathe deeply, focusing on the sensation of release in your back, hips, and shoulders.

- **Hold for 5–10 breaths.** Stay in this pose for 5–10 deep breaths, using each exhale to deepen your relaxation.
3. **Transition to Cat-Cow (Marjaryasana-Bitilasana).**
    - **Get on your hands and knees.** Come onto all fours, placing your hands directly under your shoulders and your knees under your hips. Spread your fingers wide to create a stable base.
    - **Move into Cow Pose (Bitilasana).** Inhale as you arch your back. Lift your chest, head toward the ceiling, and gently raise your tailbone. Feel the stretch along your spine and front body.
    - **Move Into Cat Pose (Marjaryasana).** Exhale as you round your back. Tuck your chin toward your chest and draw your tailbone inward, creating a gentle stretch along the back body.
    - **Repeat for 5–10 rounds.** Continue moving between Cat and Cow poses, following your breath. Inhale as you arch (Cow), and exhale as you round (Cat). Allow the movement to be slow and intentional, focusing on how your body feels in each position.
4. **Focus on your breath.** Connect your movement to your breath with each pose. Inhale deeply through your nose and exhale slowly through your mouth. This mindful breathing helps activate the parasympathetic nervous system, promoting relaxation and calming the mind.
5. **Practice for less than 30 minutes a day.** These poses can be done in under 30 minutes, making them a perfect addition to your daily routine. If you have limited time, focus on holding each pose for a few minutes, letting the benefits accumulate over time.
6. **Repeat as needed.** Integrate these poses into your day whenever you feel tension or stress building. With regular

practice, Child's Pose and Cat-Cow can help you maintain emotional balance and stay grounded throughout the day.

**Additional Recommendations**

- **Savasana (Corpse Pose).** After completing your session, lie flat on your back in Savasana for a few minutes. This pose allows you to integrate the benefits of your practice and find complete relaxation.
- **Modify if needed.** Use a blanket under your knees or forehead for extra support in the Child's Pose if needed, or take breaks if the movement feels too intense.

*Tai Chi Tranquility: A Simple Guide to Calm and Balance*

**Purpose:** Tai chi is a gentle practice that integrates mindful movement and deep breathing to enhance emotional well-being and reduce anxiety. The slow, flowing movements help you stay grounded and connected to your body while calming the mind. One effective sequence to begin with is "**Wave Hands Like Clouds,**" which promotes balance, relaxation, and mindfulness.

1. **Find a quiet, open space.** Choose a space where you have room to move comfortably. Ideally, practice tai chi in a peaceful environment, such as a quiet room or outside in nature.
2. **Begin in a standing position.**
   - **Stand with your feet shoulder-width apart.** Align your feet parallel, about hip- or shoulder-width apart.
   - **Soften your knees.** Slightly bend your knees to release tension and create a stable, relaxed stance. Keep your back straight but not rigid.

3. **Shift your weight.**
   - **Shift to one foot.** As you inhale, gently shift your weight to your right foot, feeling grounded and stable.
   - **Move with awareness.** Slowly shift your weight to your left foot as you exhale. Allow your movements to be slow and controlled, fully feeling the transfer of balance from one side to the other.
4. **"Wave Hands Like Clouds" sequence.**
   - **Hand movement.** While shifting your weight, begin to move your hands in a gentle, waving motion. Imagine your hands floating like clouds. Keep your movements fluid and soft.
   - **Coordinate with your breath.** Inhale as your hands rise gently and move to one side, and exhale as they lower and shift to the other side. Allow your breath to guide the movement.
   - **Focus on the flow.** Continue this pattern, feeling a continuous flow of energy through your body as you shift your weight and wave your hands.
5. **Mindful breathing.**
   - Inhale deeply through your nose and exhale slowly through your mouth, allowing your breath to sync with the movement. This focused breathing helps calm the nervous system, reduces stress, and promotes relaxation.
6. **Practice for 5–10 minutes or more.**
   - Continue the "Wave Hands Like Clouds" sequence for 5–10 minutes or up to 30 minutes for a full session. As you practice, focus on your body and breath, allowing anxious thoughts to melt away with each movement.
7. **Repeat daily for emotional well-being.** Incorporate this practice into your daily routine to experience long-term benefits. Even practicing tai chi for just 30 minutes a day

can significantly enhance your emotional balance, mindfulness, and overall well-being.

**Additional Recommendations**

- **Adjust for comfort.** Adjust your stance or slow the movement even further if you feel any tension or discomfort. Tai chi is meant to be gentle and calming, so modify it to suit your needs.
- **End with stillness.** After completing your tai chi sequence, take a moment to stand still with your hands by your sides. Close your eyes, breathe deeply, and feel the calm the practice has brought to your body and mind.

*Flow Freely: Dancing Your Way to Emotional Balance and Release*

**Purpose:** Dance and free movement are powerful tools for emotional expression and regulation. By moving intuitively to your favorite music, you can connect with your emotions and release tension stored in your body. This practice promotes both immediate relief and long-term emotional balance.

1. **Find a comfortable, open space.** Choose a space where you can move freely without restriction. It can be in a room, outside, or anywhere you feel comfortable to express yourself through movement.
2. **Select music that resonates with you.** Pick music that suits your mood or emotions. It could be calming, energizing, or something that helps you express feelings you need to process. Let the music guide your movement.

3. **Start with gentle movements.**
   - **Begin slowly.** Start by standing with your feet slightly apart. Allow your body to relax, and take a few deep breaths to center yourself.
   - **Tune into your body.** Begin by gently swaying or shifting your weight from one foot to the other. Let your body warm up as you gradually ease into the movement.
4. **Allow your movement to evolve.**
   - **Intuitive movement.** As the music progresses, let your body move in any way that feels right. Whether swaying, twirling, or energetic dancing, focus on how your body naturally responds to the rhythm and beats.
   - **Express your emotions.** Your movements might be slow and fluid if you feel calm. Your movements become more energetic or vigorous if you process more intense emotions. Let your body express what words can't.
5. **Stay present and focus on breath.**
   - Throughout your movement, remain mindful of your breathing. Take deep breaths as you move, allowing your breath's rhythm to sync with your body's flow. This keeps you grounded and helps you stay in the present moment.
6. **Release tension and emotions.**
   - Allow yourself to release any tension or stored emotions during your dance. Whether you're moving energetically or calmly, the process of physical expression helps release emotional and physical stress.
7. **Dance for 20–30 minutes.**
   - Move intuitively for 20–30 minutes, using this time to fully explore the range of motion and expression your body needs. You may change the music to reflect

different emotions or stay with one mood throughout the session.
8. **Repeat regularly for emotional regulation.** Incorporate dance or free movement into your routine whenever you feel emotionally overwhelmed or disconnected from your body. Regular practice will help improve your emotional balance and self-awareness over time.

**Additional Recommendations**

- **End with stillness or stretching.** After your dance session, take a moment to stand still and breathe, allowing your body to settle. You can also incorporate gentle stretching to cool down.
- **Use movement to address specific emotions.** Focus on slow, grounding movements if you feel anxious. If you're sad or angry, more energetic, fast-paced movements may help release those emotions.

## SOOTHING THE SENSES SUPPORT FOR MENTAL HEALTH

When dealing with trauma, sensory input can play a pivotal role in calming the nervous system. Sensory experiences directly engage the autonomic nervous system, particularly the parasympathetic branch, which is responsible for promoting relaxation and recovery. This connection is vital for trauma survivors who often find themselves stuck in a heightened state of alertness. By stimulating the senses, you can activate the parasympathetic system, helping to reduce stress and anxiety. Sensory grounding techniques offer an immediate way to stay present and regulate emotional responses, making them an invaluable tool for managing trauma.

*The Healing Power of Scents: Aromatherapy for Anxiety and Emotional Balance*

**Purpose:** Aromatherapy uses essential oils to promote emotional and physical healing by engaging the sense of smell. It's a powerful tool in somatic therapy for reducing anxiety, alleviating stress, and supporting trauma recovery. The olfactory system is closely linked to the brain's emotional centers, meaning inhaling calming scents can quickly promote peace and relaxation. Specific essential oils can calm the nervous system, trigger relaxation responses, and help you reconnect with your body.

1. **Choose your essential oils.** Select essential oils that target your specific needs. Some effective oils for anxiety, stress, and trauma include:
    - **Lavender:** Promotes relaxation and reduces anxiety.
    - **Chamomile:** Calms nerves and eases tension.
    - **Frankincense:** Helps alleviate feelings of stress and trauma.
    - **Ylang-Ylang:** Balances emotions and promotes a sense of peace.
    - **Bergamot:** Uplifts the mood and reduces stress.
    - **Rose:** Provides comfort and emotional healing.
2. **Decide on your application method.** There are several ways to incorporate aromatherapy into your practice:
    - **Diffusion:** An essential oil diffuser releases calming scents into the air.

- **Topical Application:** Dilute essential oils with carrier oils (like coconut or jojoba oil) and apply them to pulse points (wrists, neck, temples).
- **Inhalation:** Place a few drops on a handkerchief or inhale directly from the bottle for quick relief.
- **Bath Soak:** Add a few drops of essential oil to a warm bath to create a relaxing, immersive experience.

3. **Set the mood.** Before beginning your aromatherapy session, find a quiet, comfortable space to sit or lie down undisturbed. Dim the lights, put on soothing music, and allow yourself to fully relax in the environment.
4. **Start with deep breathing.**
   - **Inhale the aroma.** If using a diffuser, sit comfortably and close your eyes. Inhale deeply, taking in the calming scent of the essential oils. If applying topically, gently rub your wrists or neck and breathe in the aroma. Please focus on the scent and allow it to ground you in the present moment.
   - **Exhale slowly.** As you exhale, imagine releasing any tension or anxiety in your body. Repeat this for 5–10 deep breaths.
5. **Use a guided sensory meditation (optional).** For added benefit, guide yourself through a sensory meditation while inhaling the essential oils.
   - **Focus on the scent.** What memories or emotions does the scent evoke? Allow your mind to explore any thoughts that arise without judgment.
   - **Stay present.** Focus on how your body feels as you breathe deeply. The scent serves as an anchor, helping you stay connected to your body and reducing anxious or distressing thoughts.

6. **Continue for 10–20 minutes.** Remain in this state of deep breathing and sensory engagement for 10–20 minutes or longer if time allows. Let the aroma ease your nervous system and release stored emotional tension.
7. **Incorporate aromatherapy into your daily routine.** Aromatherapy can be used throughout the day as part of your daily routine for ongoing stress relief. Diffuse oils in your home or workspace, apply them during moments of high stress or use them before bed to improve sleep and relaxation.

**Additional Recommendations**

- **Rotate oils for different effects.** Try different essential oils based on your emotional needs. Use lavender or chamomile to calm anxiety before sleep or bergamot and ylang-ylang to uplift your mood during the day.
- **Ensure proper dilution.** Always dilute oils with a carrier oil to prevent skin irritation when applying oils topically. A good ratio is 2–3 drops of essential oil per teaspoon of carrier oil.

*The Healing Soundtrack: Music Therapy for Emotional Balance*

**Purpose:** Music therapy is a powerful sensory technique that can create emotional balance, reduce stress, and help process trauma. Music profoundly affects mood and emotions, making it a valuable tool in somatic therapy. Using music intentionally can soothe the nervous system, manage emotional responses, and foster healing.

1. **Choose your music.** Select music that resonates with your emotional state or the goal of your session. Here are some types of music to consider:
   - **Calming Music:** Soft, instrumental, or natural sounds (e.g., rain, ocean waves) to promote relaxation.
   - **Uplifting Music:** Melodic, cheerful tunes to lift your mood and provide emotional relief.
   - **Deep, Reflective Music:** Classical or ambient music for introspective sessions aimed at processing emotions and trauma.
2. **Experiment with different genres** to find what best suits your needs.
3. **Set the stage.** Create a comfortable environment to fully engage with the music. Sit or lie down in a quiet space, dim the lights if necessary, and ensure no distractions. This will help you focus solely on the therapeutic experience.
4. **Start with deep breathing.**
   - **Inhale deeply.** Before playing the music, take a few deep breaths to calm your mind and body. Inhale through your nose for a count of four, and exhale through your mouth for a count of six.
   - **Let go of tension.** With each exhale, consciously release any tension in your body. This will help prepare you to receive the calming effects of the music.
5. **Engage with the music.**
   - **Press play.** Start your chosen playlist and close your eyes if that feels comfortable. Let the music wash over you, noticing how it affects your emotions and body.
   - **Focus on your breath.** As you listen, continue to breathe slowly and deeply. Let the rhythm and melody guide your breath and ground you in the present moment.

- **Observe emotional reactions.** Pay attention to how the music impacts your emotions. Do certain notes or instruments evoke specific feelings? Allow yourself to feel whatever emotions arise without judgment.
6. **Use music to process trauma or stress.**
    - **Reflect on emotions.** If you're processing trauma or stress, focus on how the music can help express or release those emotions. Let the music be a tool for emotional expression. For instance, faster tempos allow you to release pent-up energy, while slower, soothing sounds can help you calm down.
    - **Body scan with music.** You can incorporate a body scan, noticing any tension in your body as you listen. Let the music guide your awareness to areas of tension, using its calming effects to help release tightness or stress.
7. **Play for 20–30 minutes.** Engage with your music therapy session for at least 20–30 minutes, giving yourself ample time to relax into the experience. Whether you're processing trauma or simply looking to relieve stress, this time will allow the music to take full effect.
8. **Incorporate music into your daily routine.** Music therapy can be a powerful daily tool. Use calming music in the background while you work, play relaxing tunes before bed, or choose energizing songs in the morning to start your day with emotional balance. Over time, this practice can enhance your emotional regulation and overall well-being.

**Additional Recommendations**

- **Vocalize if it feels right.** If you're moved to sing or hum along with the music, let yourself do so. Vocalizing can enhance emotional release and deepen the connection with the music.
- **Change the tempo to match your needs.** Use slow, soothing music when you need calm and more upbeat, rhythmic tunes when you need to release energy or process difficult emotions.

*Tactile Stimulation for Emotional Balance*

**Purpose:** Tactile stimulation is a powerful sensory technique that helps ground you in the present moment by focusing on physical sensations. Whether you're holding a smooth stone, a piece of fabric, or a stress ball, the act of engaging with these objects can provide immediate relief from anxiety, trauma, or dissociation. This simple, practical method offers a tangible way to manage stress and promote long-term emotional regulation.

1. **Select your tactile object.** Identify an object that brings you comfort or helps ground you. Some effective choices include:
    - **Smooth Stone:** Its solid, cool texture can provide a calming effect.
    - **Piece of Fabric:** Soft fabric or textured cloth can be soothing to the touch.
    - **Stress Ball:** Squeezing a stress ball helps release tension and provides physical engagement.
2. **Choose an object** that resonates with you and can easily be carried throughout your day.

3. **Keep your object accessible.** Carry your tactile object with you, especially if you anticipate stressful situations or moments of high anxiety. Place it in your pocket or bag or on your desk for quick access.
4. **Engage with the object during stressful moments.**
   - **Hold the object.** When you feel anxious, overwhelmed, or dissociated, take the object in your hand.
   - **Focus on the texture.** Pay close attention to the object's texture, weight, and temperature. If it's a smooth stone, feel the cool surface and notice its shape. If it's fabric, focus on its softness or texture.
   - **Press or squeeze.** If using a stress ball, gently press or squeeze the ball in your hand, releasing muscle tension while keeping your mind focused on the sensation.
5. **Stay present with the sensations.**
   - **Stay grounded.** As you engage with the object, focus on how your body feels in the moment. This physical sensation helps bring your attention back to the present, interrupting any spiraling thoughts or anxiety.
   - **Breathe deeply.** Take slow, deep breaths as you engage with the tactile object. Inhale through your nose and exhale through your mouth, using the physical sensation to anchor your breath.
6. **Use tactile stimulation during anxiety or dissociation.** Tactile stimulation is particularly effective during moments of high anxiety or dissociation. Holding the object provides a tangible point of focus, helping you feel more connected to your body and the present moment.
7. **Practice for immediate relief.** Continue holding and focusing on the object for as long as needed. Most people experience relief after just a few minutes of tactile engagement. Still, you can continue as long as it feels helpful.

8. **Incorporate tactile stimulation into your daily routine.** Integrate this technique into your daily life to manage stress. Whether you're in a meeting, commuting, or at home, holding your grounding object can help maintain a sense of calm and balance.

**Additional Recommendations**

- **Experiment with different objects.** Try using various objects—smooth, rough, soft, or firm—until you find one that best suits your needs.
- **Use alongside other grounding techniques.** Combine tactile stimulation with breathing exercises, sensory grounding, or movement techniques for a more comprehensive approach to managing stress and anxiety.

Consider the story of Janelle, a veteran who managed PTSD symptoms through aromatherapy. By using lavender essential oil, Janelle found that she could quickly calm her mind and regulate her emotions during moments of distress. Another example is Gloria, an abuse survivor who found comfort in music therapy. By listening to calming music, Gloria was able to process her emotions and find relief from her trauma. These stories highlight the transformative power of sensory techniques in managing trauma responses.

Combining different somatic therapies offers a more comprehensive approach to healing, allowing you to address both your mind and body in moments of distress. By incorporating various techniques—such as breathing exercises, tactile stimulation, movement, and grounding practices—you can tailor your practice to meet your specific emotional needs in the moment. As you track your progress and observe how your body and emotions respond to each method, you will begin to see which combinations work best for managing anxiety, stress, or trauma. This personalized approach empowers you to take control of your healing journey, offering a more effective, holistic way to regain emotional balance and resilience. Through consistent practice and mindful adjustments, these techniques can become powerful tools to navigate and transform your emotional landscape.

# 4

# EMOTIONAL AND PHYSICAL REGULATION THROUGH THE AUTONOMIC NERVOUS SYSTEM

*"The vagus nerve is the body's highway to healing, connecting the brain, heart, and gut in a symphony of self-regulation."*

— UNKNOWN

Imagine waking up every day feeling like your body is stuck in survival mode. Your heart races, your muscles are tense, and you can't seem to relax no matter what you do. This was the reality for Ivan, a veteran struggling with PTSD. Traditional therapy had helped him understand his trauma, but his body still felt like it was on high alert. That's when we turned to understanding his autonomic nervous system (ANS) and how it could be harnessed to bring him the calm he desperately needed.

## THE POWER OF THE VAGUS NERVE

The autonomic nervous system (ANS) is a part of your peripheral nervous system that regulates unconscious body functions like heartbeat, blood flow, breathing, and digestion. Essentially, it acts as your body's autopilot, ensuring these processes run smoothly without you having to think about them. The ANS plays a crucial role in maintaining a balance between stress and relaxation, helping your body respond to environmental changes and return to a state of equilibrium. It operates by receiving information from your surroundings and other parts of your body and then adjusting internal processes to maintain stability.

The ANS is divided into three branches: the sympathetic nervous system, the parasympathetic nervous system, and the enteric nervous system. Each branch has a specific role in regulating your body's functions. The sympathetic nervous system is often called the "fight-or-flight" system. In contrast, the parasympathetic nervous system is known as the "rest-and-digest" system. It helps your body relax, digest food, and recover after periods of stress. When this system is activated, your heart rate slows, digestion is stimulated, and your body becomes calm and restored. This is where the vagus nerve comes into play. The vagus nerve is a long cranial nerve that runs from the brainstem to the abdomen, connecting to various organs along the way. It plays a crucial role in activating the parasympathetic system, promoting relaxation, and reducing stress. Techniques such as deep breathing, meditation, and vagus nerve stimulation can help activate this system, aiding in emotional and physical recovery.

The enteric nervous system, often called the "second brain," controls the gastrointestinal tract and digestion. There is a significant connection between gut health and mental health. Stress can disrupt digestion, leading to issues like irritable bowel syndrome (IBS) and other gastrointestinal problems. Conversely, a balanced gut can improve emotional well-being. The gut-brain axis highlights this connection, showing that the health of your gut can influence your mood and overall mental health. Maintaining a healthy diet, managing stress, and using probiotics can improve gut health, enhancing your emotional well-being.

Balancing the sympathetic and parasympathetic systems is crucial for both mental and physical health. When these systems are in harmony, your body can effectively manage and recover from stress. Techniques like mindfulness, deep breathing, and somatic exercises are essential in restoring this balance. For example, practicing mindfulness helps you stay present and reduce stress, while deep breathing activates the parasympathetic system, promoting relaxation. Somatic exercises, which focus on bodily sensations, also play a role in calming the nervous system and releasing stored tension. By incorporating these practices into your daily routine, you can achieve a state of balance and well-being, much like Ivan did in his journey to recovery.

## FIGHT OR FLIGHT STRESS RESPONSES

When stress strikes, your body springs into action, preparing you to face the challenge head-on. This is known as the fight-or-flight response, a vital survival mechanism. During stressful situations, the sympathetic nervous system (SNS) takes the lead. It releases adrenaline and cortisol, essential stress hormones that boost your alertness and energy. Your heart rate spikes, blood pressure rises, and breathing quickens. This immediate activation is driven by the hypothalamic-pituitary-adrenal (HPA) axis, which signals your adrenal glands to pump out these hormones. The result is a cascade of physiological changes designed to prepare you for action.

Several notable changes occur as your body gears up for fight or flight. Your heart races to pump more blood, delivering oxygen and nutrients to muscles primed for action. Rapid breathing increases oxygen intake, fueling your heightened state. Muscles tense, preparing for quick, powerful movements. Pupils dilate to enhance vision, allowing you to spot potential threats more efficiently. These physical changes are crucial for short-term survival but can become problematic if they persist. Chronic activation of the sympathetic nervous system keeps your body in a state of high alert, leading to anxiety, high blood pressure, and digestive issues over time.

Living in a constant state of stress wreaks havoc on your body. Chronic sympathetic activation drains your energy and leaves you feeling perpetually exhausted. Anxiety becomes a constant companion as your body remains on edge, ready to react to perceived threats. High blood pressure, a common consequence, increases the risk of heart disease and other serious health conditions. Digestive problems, such as irritable bowel syndrome (IBS), often arise as prolonged stress disrupts normal gut function. The importance of addressing chronic stress cannot be overstated. Left unchecked, it leads to burnout, a state of physical, emotional, and mental exhaustion that can be difficult to recover from.

After prolonged stress, your body may shift from fight-or-flight to a freeze-fawn response. This occurs when the stress becomes too overwhelming, and the body can no longer sustain the high-alert state. In the freeze response, your body essentially shuts down, leaving you feeling numb, detached, or immobilized. In the fawn response, you instinctively prioritize appeasing others or avoiding conflict as a means of maintaining safety. Both responses are protective mechanisms aimed at minimizing harm when active resistance or escape is no longer perceived as viable. While they can serve as temporary coping strategies, staying in these states for extended periods can exacerbate feelings of helplessness and depression.

## THE VAGUS NERVE'S ROLL IN REST AND RECHARGE

The parasympathetic nervous system (PNS) is like your body's internal brake system, helping you slow down and recover after periods of stress. It works to counterbalance the fight-or-flight response by calming your heart rate, stimulating digestion, and restoring a state of relaxation. This restorative system is crucial for your overall well-being, preventing stress from taking a long-term toll on your health. A central player in this system is the vagus nerve, the longest cranial nerve, which acts as a communication bridge between your brain and major organs, such as the heart, lungs, and digestive tract.

The vagus nerve regulates critical functions like heart rhythm, breathing, and digestion. It slows your heart rate during rest, counters the effects of stress and anxiety, and promotes relaxation.

Its connection to the digestive system supports gut motility and enzyme release, strengthening the gut-brain axis and highlighting how stress and emotions affect digestion. This intricate network ensures your body operates in harmony, maintaining balance and resilience.

One of the most effective ways to activate the vagus nerve—and, in turn, the parasympathetic system—is through targeted techniques like deep breathing, mindfulness, or even humming. Deep breathing engages the diaphragm, stimulating the vagus nerve and calming your heart rate. Practices like yoga and tai chi combine breathwork and gentle movement, enhancing vagus nerve activity and reducing stress. Social engagement, such as connecting with loved ones or participating in hobbies, also supports vagus nerve activation by fostering feelings of safety and connection.

Balancing the sympathetic and parasympathetic systems is vital for managing stress and promoting recovery. Without engaging the PNS, chronic stress can lead to burnout and emotional exhaustion. Regularly incorporating vagus nerve-stimulating practices into your daily routine helps maintain equilibrium, improving emotional regulation, cardiovascular health, and digestion while building resilience against stress. Understanding the parasympathetic system's and vagus nerve's role empowers you to unlock relaxation and support long-term well-being.

## THE ROLE OF GLUTAMATE IN BALANCING THE BRAIN

When discussing emotional and physical regulation through the autonomic nervous system (ANS), understanding the role of **glutamate**, the brain's primary excitatory neurotransmitter, is essential. Glutamate acts like the brain's accelerator, driving critical functions such as learning, memory, and neural communication.  However, just as an overworked car engine risks overheating, too much glutamate in the system can lead to **glutamate overload**, a state where excessive levels of this neurotransmitter overstimulate neurons, leading to cellular damage and impaired function.

Under chronic stress, the body's fight-or-flight response, driven by the sympathetic nervous system, can trigger excessive glutamate release. This excitatory surge helps you respond to immediate danger but can become harmful when stress is prolonged. High glutamate levels can result in **excitotoxicity**, a condition where neurons are overstimulated to the point of damage or death. This process is linked to heightened anxiety, depression, cognitive impairments, and even physical issues like chronic inflammation. Over time, glutamate overload can disrupt the balance between the sympathetic and parasympathetic systems, perpetuating a cycle of stress and emotional dysregulation.

Thankfully, strategies that regulate the ANS can help reduce glutamate overload, promoting brain health and emotional resilience. Techniques such as **somatic therapy**, **vagus nerve stimulation (VNS)**, and **heart rate variability (HRV) biofeedback** are particularly effective. These approaches activate the parasympathetic nervous system, the body's natural "braking" mechanism, which counteracts the excitatory effects of stress and glutamate. For instance:

- **Somatic Therapy:** Grounding exercises, mindful movement, and body awareness practices calm the nervous system, reducing stress-induced glutamate release.
- **Vagus Nerve Stimulation:** Practices like diaphragmatic breathing, humming, or cold exposure stimulate the vagus nerve, promoting relaxation by increasing the release of inhibitory neurotransmitters like gamma-aminobutyric acid (GABA), which counterbalances glutamate.
- **HRV Biofeedback:** Improving vagal tone through HRV biofeedback enhances stress adaptability, helping the body switch more efficiently from a state of stress to relaxation.

These techniques not only regulate glutamate levels but also protect neurons from excitotoxic damage. By incorporating these practices into your daily routine, you can maintain a healthy balance of neurotransmitters, support emotional and physical well-being, and cultivate resilience against stress. Understanding glutamate's role in the brain underscores the importance of managing stress through ANS regulation, paving the way for a healthier, more balanced nervous system.

## VAGAL TONE IS THE SECRET TO EMOTIONAL RESILIENCE

The vagus nerve plays a crucial role in regulating emotional and physical responses, acting as a bridge between your brain and body. High vagal tone, a measure of the vagus nerve's activity, is key to stress resilience and emotional balance. When vagal tone is high, your body efficiently shifts from stress to relaxation, reducing symptoms of anxiety and depression. This adaptability supports faster recovery from stress and fosters a sense of calm, making it easier to manage conditions like PTSD and chronic stress.

On the other hand, low vagal tone is associated with difficulty transitioning from stress to relaxation, leading to heightened anxiety, depression, and chronic inflammation. This state can leave you feeling constantly on edge, with a weakened immune response and increased vulnerability to illness. Improving vagal tone helps break this cycle, enhancing your ability to regulate emotions and manage stress effectively.

Heart rate variability (HRV), the variation in time between heartbeats, is a reliable indicator of vagal tone. Higher HRV reflects better stress adaptability and overall resilience. Techniques such as diaphragmatic breathing, cold exposure, and mindfulness can stimulate the vagus nerve and improve vagal tone. These practices not only enhance emotional regulation but also boost physical health, including better digestion, a stronger immune system, and improved heart health.

By incorporating vagal tone-boosting practices into your daily routine, you can foster a balanced nervous system, strengthen your stress resilience, and support both emotional and physical well-being.

## THE VAGUS NERVE TRANSFORMS HEALING FROM TRAUMA

Dr. Stephen Porges first introduced the Polyvagal Theory in 1994. This theory offered a new perspective on how the vagus nerve plays a critical role in regulating emotions, stress responses, and social engagement. It has since become foundational in understanding the connection between the autonomic nervous system and emotional regulation, particularly in the context of trauma and therapy. The theory posits that the vagus nerve plays a crucial role in helping the body transition between states of stress and calm. Porges explains how this complex system influences our emotional regulation and overall well-being by examining the different branches of the vagus nerve. His groundbreaking research has significant implications for how we approach trauma therapy today.

Polyvagal Theory focuses on the vagus nerve's ability to help the body navigate between states of stress and relaxation. When you experience stress, your body responds by activating the sympathetic nervous system, preparing you for fight or flight. However, the vagus nerve has the power to counteract this response, guiding you back to a state of calm. This shift is essential for emotional regulation. By understanding how the vagus nerve contributes to this process, we gain valuable insights into managing anxiety, PTSD, and other stress-related conditions. Techniques stimulating the vagus nerve, such as deep breathing and mindfulness, can help facilitate this transition, promoting emotional stability.

One of the most intriguing aspects of Polyvagal Theory is the concept of the "social engagement system." This system, which is part of the vagus nerve, helps you feel safe and connected to others. When the social engagement system is activated, it promotes feelings of safety and facilitates social interactions. This is why you might feel calmer and more at ease in the presence of trusted friends or family. The social engagement system helps regulate your emotions, making it easier to manage stress and anxiety. By fostering positive social connections, you can enhance the activation of this system, supporting your overall emotional well-being.

For trauma therapists, Polyvagal Theory offers valuable insights into creating interventions that promote safety and emotional regulation. Therapists can develop techniques that help clients feel more secure and grounded by understanding how the vagus nerve influences emotional states. For example, incorporating practices stimulating the vagus nerve, such as gentle touch or rhythmic movement, can help clients regulate their emotions and reduce trauma symptoms. These interventions create a sense of safety, allowing clients to process their trauma without becoming overwhelmed. Polyvagal Theory provides a framework for understanding and addressing the complex interplay between the nervous system and emotional health.

## IMPROVING VAGAL TONE FOR A BALANCED NERVOUS SYSTEM

Polyvagal Theory offers practical ways to improve emotional regulation through specific exercises stimulating the vagus nerve. One effective technique is diaphragmatic breathing. This involves taking deep breaths that fully engage your diaphragm. When you inhale deeply, your belly should rise, and as you exhale, it should fall. This type of breathing can be done anywhere and helps activate the parasympathetic nervous system, promoting a sense of calm and relaxation. Another powerful method is cold exposure, such as taking a cold shower or immersing your face in cold water. This brief exposure to cold stimulates the vagus nerve, helping to reset your nervous system and improve emotional balance.

Vocal exercises like humming or chanting also offer significant benefits for emotional regulation. These exercises create vibrations that stimulate the vagus nerve, helping to calm your mind and body. For instance, humming a favorite tune or chanting "OM" can be easily integrated into your daily routine. These practices reduce stress and improve heart rate variability (HRV), a key indicator of your body's ability to handle stress. Regularly engaging in these exercises helps build long-term nervous system resilience, making it easier to manage anxiety and emotional fluctuations.

Incorporating these techniques into your daily routine is crucial for building resilience and maintaining emotional health. Creating a habit of vagus nerve activation supports overall well-being and helps manage stress more effectively. For example, starting your day with a few minutes of deep breathing can set a positive tone, while ending the day with a cold shower can help you unwind. Consistent practice of these methods trains your nervous system to respond more adaptively to stress, reducing the impact of daily challenges.

Consider the case of Angie, a trauma survivor who struggled with chronic anxiety. By integrating Polyvagal-informed techniques into her routine, she experienced significant improvements. She practiced diaphragmatic breathing each morning, took a cold shower in the evening, and hummed her favorite tune during stressful moments. Over time, Angie noticed that her anxiety levels decreased, and she felt more emotionally balanced. Similarly, Tom, a veteran with PTSD, found relief through these exercises. He incorporated deep breathing and cold exposure into his daily routine, leading to a marked reduction in his PTSD symptoms and an improved sense of well-being.

These real-life examples highlight the transformative power of vagus nerve stimulation. For many, these simple yet effective practices can make a substantial difference in managing stress and improving emotional health.

Understanding and applying Polyvagal Theory offers a roadmap to enhancing emotional regulation. The next chapter will delve deeper into integrating these practices with other therapeutic techniques for holistic healing.

# 5

# VAGUS NERVE RESET FOR EMOTIONAL CONTROL AND INNER PEACE

> *"Activating the vagus nerve is like tuning the strings of an instrument; it brings the body back into harmony and balance."*
>
> — DEB DANA

Picture yourself in a moment of overwhelming stress. Maybe the aftermath of a difficult conversation or the relentless worry keeps you up at night. Your heart races and thumps so loud you can hear it in your ears, your breath becomes shallow, and a sense of unease takes over. These physical reactions are not just in your head; they are deeply rooted in your body's nervous system. Understanding and utilizing vagus nerve stimulation (VNS) can make a significant difference. By learning to activate the vagus nerve, you can tap into your body's natural ability to calm itself, offering a powerful tool for managing emotions and reducing stress.

Remember to grab your free bonus worksheets by SCANNING THE BARCODE BELOW! These tools are designed to enhance the exercises in this chapter and guide you on your healing journey.

YOUR GUIDE TO VAGUS NERVE STIMULATION

Vagus nerve stimulation (VNS) offers a practical, noninvasive way to improve emotional regulation and build resilience against stress. These techniques can be seamlessly incorporated into your daily routine, requiring no more than 30 minutes daily. Engaging in VNS helps your body shift from stress to relaxation, making it an invaluable tool for mental well-being. Whether you're dealing with anxiety, depression, PTSD, or the everyday stresses of life, VNS provides a straightforward method to support your emotional health.

Several methods stimulate the vagus nerve, each offering unique benefits. Breathwork, for instance, involves deep, intentional breathing exercises that activate the parasympathetic nervous system, promoting relaxation. Cold exposure, such as taking a short cold shower or placing your face in cold water, can also stimulate the vagus nerve and enhance stress resilience. Vocal exercises, including humming, chanting, or singing, use vibrations to activate the vagus nerve and calm the nervous system. Lastly, certain dietary practices, like consuming anti-inflammatory foods and staying hydrated, support overall vagal tone and nervous system function. The following sections will explore these approaches in more detail, providing a versatile toolkit for emotional regulation.

One of the most compelling aspects of VNS is its accessibility. You do not need any special equipment or training to get started. These techniques can be performed in the comfort of your home, making incorporating them into your daily life easy. These practices are practical and effective, whether a few minutes of deep breathing in the morning, a quick cold shower after a workout, or humming along to your favorite song during your commute. Their simplicity and ease of use make VNS a valuable tool for consistent emotional and stress management.

The science behind vagus nerve stimulation is robust and well-documented. For example, a study published in the *American Journal of Psychiatry* found that VNS significantly reduced symptoms of treatment-resistant depression (Aaronson T.L. et al., 2017). Another study highlighted in the *Journal of Traumatic Stress* showed that VNS could help reduce PTSD symptoms by calming the nervous system and promoting a sense of safety (Langmuir J. et al., 2012). These findings validate the effectiveness of VNS in managing trauma and anxiety, offering hope and relief to those who incorporate these techniques into their lives.

## THE TRANSFORMATIVE POWER OF DEEP BREATHING

Deep breathing is a simple yet powerful tool for enhancing emotional well-being. Slow, intentional breaths improve vagal tone by activating the parasympathetic nervous system, which is responsible for relaxation and recovery, helping your body manage stress and regulate emotions more effectively. This balance between the fight-or-flight and rest-and-digest systems is key to maintaining emotional stability and resilience.

Deep breathing positively influences heart rate variability (HRV), a measure of the balance between your sympathetic and parasympathetic systems. Higher HRV is linked to better stress management and emotional regulation. Incorporating these techniques into your daily routine can help reduce anxiety, improve emotional balance, and promote overall well-being—all in just a few minutes a day.

These step-by-step breathing exercises are designed to calm the nervous system, increase HRV, and bring a sense of calm to your body and mind. Paired with downloadable worksheets, they provide a structured way to track your progress and build resilience. Start practicing today to unlock lasting balance and peace.

### Diaphragmatic Breathing (Belly Breathing)

**Purpose:** Diaphragmatic breathing promotes relaxation, reduces stress, and enhances vagal tone. It is an effective method for improving oxygen exchange and calming the nervous system. Practice this technique for 5–10 minutes daily to experience noticeable emotional regulation and overall well-being improvements.

1. **Find a comfortable position.** Sit or lie down in a relaxed position. You can do this exercise in bed, on the couch, or in a chair with your back supported.
2. **Place your hands.** Rest one hand on your chest and the other on your abdomen to help monitor your breathing.
3. **Inhale deeply.** Breathe in through your nose, allowing your abdomen to rise while keeping your chest still. Focus on filling your lower lungs.
4. **Exhale slowly.** Breathe through your mouth, feeling your abdomen fall as you release your breath.
5. **Repeat for 5–10 minutes.** Continue this cycle for 5–10 minutes, focusing on slow, deep breaths.

### Coherent Breathing

**Purpose:** Coherent breathing helps balance the autonomic nervous system, reduces anxiety, and increases heart rate variability (HRV). Maintaining a consistent breathing rate can quickly achieve a calm and focused state. Practice for 5–10 minutes a day.

1. **Get comfortable.** Sit comfortably with your feet flat on the floor or lie down in a quiet space.
2. **Breathe in.** Inhale slowly through your nose for a count of six.

3. **Breathe out.** Exhale gently through your mouth for a count of six.
4. **Establish rhythm.** Continue breathing in and out, maintaining this rhythm of approximately five breaths per minute.
5. **Practice for 5–10 minutes.** Aim to keep your breathing rate consistent for the entire practice.

*Resonant Frequency Breathing*

**Purpose:** Resonant frequency breathing helps maximize heart rate variability (HRV), promoting emotional resilience and calming the nervous system. This technique involves finding your unique breath rate that feels most calming. Practice for 5–10 minutes a day.

1. **Relax your body.** Sit or lie down in a comfortable, quiet space.
2. **Begin coherent breathing.** Start by inhaling for 5–6 seconds and exhaling for 5–6 seconds.
3. **Find your resonant frequency.** Experiment by slightly adjusting the inhale and exhale durations until you find the breath rate that feels the most calming and natural.
4. **Maintain your rhythm.** Once you've found your optimal breathing rate, continue breathing at this pace for the remainder of the session.
5. **Practice for 5–10 minutes.** Focus on this breathing rhythm to fully engage your parasympathetic nervous system.

### Extended Exhalation Breathing

**Purpose:** Extended exhalation breathing helps deepen relaxation by slowing the heart rate and activating the vagus nerve. This technique is particularly effective for reducing anxiety. Practice for 3–5 minutes a day or whenever you need quick relaxation.

1. **Find a comfortable position:** Sit or lie down, ensuring you're in a quiet and comfortable environment.
2. **Inhale for four counts.** Breathe in through your nose for a slow count of four.
3. **Exhale for six to eight counts.** Breathe out through your mouth for a longer count of six or eight.
4. **Focus on the exhale.** Make sure your exhale is longer than your inhale to trigger deeper relaxation.
5. **Continue for 3–5 minutes.** Repeat this breathing pattern, allowing your body to relax more deeply with each extended exhale.

### 4-7-8 Breathing Technique

**Purpose:** The 4-7-8 breathing technique is powerful for quickly reducing stress and promoting sleep. It also enhances vagal tone and supports emotional regulation. Practice this technique for 2–4 minutes, especially during moments of stress or before bed.

1. **Sit comfortably.** Find a seated position with your back straight. Place the tip of your tongue behind your upper front teeth.
2. **Inhale for four counts.** Breathe in quietly through your nose for a count of four.
3. **Hold for seven counts.** Hold your breath for a count of seven.

4. **Exhale for eight counts.** Exhale entirely through your mouth for a count of eight, making a "whoosh" sound as you do.
5. **Repeat for 2–4 minutes.** To start, perform this breathing cycle for four rounds, gradually increasing as you become more comfortable with the technique.

Regular breathwork offers numerous psychological benefits. It can reduce anxiety, improve focus, and help manage panic attacks. Engaging in these exercises can create a sense of emotional stability and build resilience over time. Deep breathing helps calm the mind, making concentrating and staying present easier. It also provides a tool for managing intense emotions, allowing you to ground yourself and regain control during stressful moments.

Making deep breathing a habit is easier than you think. Start by setting aside time in the morning to practice, which will help set a calm tone for your day. Incorporate breathing exercises into moments of stress, such as during a difficult meeting or before a challenging task. Practicing before bed can also promote better sleep. Integrating these techniques into your daily routine allows you to create a consistent and beneficial practice that supports your overall well-being.

## BUILD RESILIENCE WITH COLD EXPOSURE THERAPY

Imagine the invigorating shock of stepping into a cold shower on a brisk morning. This simple act can do more than wake you up; it can stimulate your vagus nerve and activate your parasympathetic nervous system. Cold exposure triggers a response in your body that promotes resilience to stress. When cold water touches your skin, it signals to your brain, activating the vagus nerve. This results in a calming effect, helping to regulate your emotions and reduce stress. The science behind this involves the body's natural response to cold, which includes a brief activation of the sympathetic nervous system followed by a stronger, longer-lasting activation of the parasympathetic system. This helps to increase your ability to manage stress and improve emotional regulation.

Cold exposure offers numerous mental and physical benefits. It can reduce inflammation, which is often linked to chronic stress and mental health issues like depression and anxiety. By lowering inflammation, you may notice an improvement in your overall mood and energy levels. Cold exposure also boosts immune function, making you more resilient to illnesses. The invigorating effect of cold water can enhance your mood by increasing the levels of endorphins and norepinephrine in your brain. These chemicals are natural mood boosters, helping you feel more alert and cheerful. Regular practice can lead to better energy levels throughout the day, making it easier to manage daily stressors.

*Gradual Cold Showers*

**Purpose:** Cold showers are an easy way to begin incorporating cold exposure into your daily routine. They help build resilience, stimulate circulation, and activate the parasympathetic nervous system.

1. **Start with warm water.** Begin your shower with warm water to ease into the process and relax your muscles.

2. **Gradually reduce the temperature.** After a minute or two, slowly decrease the water temperature until it becomes cold. Start with water that feels cool but not unbearable.
3. **Time your exposure.** At first, stand under the cold water for 30 seconds to 1 minute. Gradually increase the duration as your body adjusts to the cold.
4. **Breathe deeply.** Focus on slow, deep breaths as you expose yourself to the cold water. This will help reduce any initial discomfort and promote relaxation.
5. **Increase duration gradually.** Over several days or weeks, try to increase the length of your cold showers by 15–30 seconds as your body becomes more acclimated.

*Face Immersion in Cold Water*

**Purpose:** Face immersion is a gentle way to practice cold exposure without the intensity of a full cold shower. It helps stimulate the vagus nerve and promotes a calming effect.

1. **Prepare the basin.** Fill a basin or sink with cold water. You can add ice to make it colder, but ensure the water temperature is tolerable.
2. **Immerse your face.** Lower your face into the cold water and hold it there for 10–15 seconds. Breathe normally through your nose.
3. **Repeat the process.** Lift your face out of the water, take a few deep breaths, and then repeat the immersion 2–3 times.
4. **Adjust as needed.** As you get more comfortable, you can increase the duration of each immersion by 5 seconds, but don't overdo it.

*Ice Baths*

**Purpose:** Ice baths are a more advanced form of cold exposure that can build resilience, reduce inflammation, and improve recovery. Start slow and always proceed with caution.

1. **Prepare the ice bath.** Fill a bathtub with cold water, then gradually add ice until the water reaches a temperature of around 50–60°F (10–15°C).
2. **Start with short immersions.** Begin by submerging yourself in the ice bath for 1–2 minutes. Keep your head above the water to avoid cold shock.
3. **Listen to your body.** Pay attention to how your body feels. If you experience discomfort beyond initial coldness or start to shiver uncontrollably, exit the bath immediately.
4. **Have someone nearby**. Always ensure that someone is present when trying ice baths for the first time to monitor your safety.
5. **Gradually increase time.** You can gradually increase to longer immersions, but never push past what feels comfortable.

*Safety Tips for Cold Exposure*

Cold exposure can be powerful but should always be approached with caution. Here are a few safety tips to keep in mind:

- **Start gradually.** Allow your body time to acclimatize to cold exposure.
- **Listen to your body.** Never push past discomfort or shivering, as this can signify your body reaching its cold limit.

- **Avoid submerging your head.** Keep your head out of the water in ice baths to prevent shock.
- **Consult a healthcare provider.** If you have any pre-existing health conditions, it is essential to consult a healthcare professional before starting a cold exposure routine.

*Final Step: Track Your Progress*

Tracking your progress can be incredibly helpful in understanding the benefits of cold exposure. Note how you feel before and after each session, paying attention to your mood, energy levels, and any changes in stress or anxiety. This practice will help you see the cumulative benefits and keep you motivated. Over time, you might notice improvements in resilience, a more balanced mood, and increased energy. Cold exposure is more than just a physical practice; it is a holistic approach to enhancing mental and emotional well-being.

## HUMMING AND GARGLING STIMULATES THE VAGUS NERVE

Imagine the soothing hum of a favorite tune resonating through your body, bringing a sense of calm and peace. This pleasant experience is also a powerful way to stimulate your vagus nerve. Vocal exercises like humming and chanting use vibrations to engage the vagus nerve, activating the parasympathetic nervous system. These vibrations travel through your vocal cords and into your chest, promoting relaxation and improving emotional regulation. Similarly, gargling creates a gentle, rhythmic stimulation through the vocal cords that activates the vagus nerve. Whether humming a tune or gargling at the bathroom sink, both techniques help lower stress levels, making it easier to manage emotions and find a sense of calm.

The benefits of gargling and humming for mental health are substantial. These simple techniques offer immediate stress relief by stimulating the vagus nerve, which activates the parasympathetic system. This process helps lower heart rate, reduce blood pressure, and calm the nervous system, providing practical tools for managing anxiety and improving mood. The accessibility of these methods makes them easy to incorporate into your daily routine, offering quick, effective ways to regulate your emotions—whether you're dealing with work stress, trauma, or everyday challenges.

*Humming*

**Purpose:** Humming is one of the easiest and most accessible methods for vagus nerve stimulation. The vibrations from humming help calm your nervous system and promote relaxation.

1. **Find a comfortable position.** Sit or lie down in a relaxed, quiet space where you won't be disturbed.
2. **Close your eyes and breathe.** Take a few deep breaths to center yourself.
3. **Start humming a tune.** Hum any simple tune that feels pleasant to you, such as a song or even a single tone. Focus on the vibrations you feel in your chest and throat as you hum.

4. **Focus on the vibration.** To enhance the calming effect, pay attention to how the vibrations travel through your body, especially around your chest and throat.
5. **Repeat for 3–5 minutes.** Hum for a few minutes, adjusting your pitch or tone if it feels right.

*Chanting "OM"*

**Purpose:** Chanting "OM" is a traditional vocal exercise that creates deep, resonant vibrations to stimulate the vagus nerve. This method promotes a deep sense of calm and connection to your body.

1. **Sit comfortably.** Find a seated position with your spine straight, either on the floor or in a chair.
2. **Take a deep breath.** Inhale deeply through your nose.
3. **Chant "OM" slowly.** As you exhale, chant "OM" slowly, allowing the sound to resonate for as long as possible. Focus on the vibrations it creates in your chest and throat.
4. **Repeat the chant.** Take another deep breath and repeat the chant several times, paying attention to the soothing effect of the vibrations.
5. **Continue for 3–5 minutes.** Chant for several minutes, letting yourself relax more deeply with each repetition.

*Gargling*

**Purpose:** Gargling is another simple method for stimulating the vagus nerve through gentle vibrations created in your throat. By engaging the parasympathetic nervous system, gargling helps to reduce stress, regulate emotions, and promote relaxation. It's easy to practice and can be done multiple times a day for consistent emotional support.

1. **Prepare a sip of water.** Take a small sip of water, ensuring it's at a comfortable temperature—not too hot or too cold.
2. **Tilt your head back.** Tilt your head back so the water reaches the back of your throat.
3. **Start gargling.** Begin to gargle, creating a steady, gentle vibration in your throat as you exhale through your mouth. Focus on keeping the sound rhythmic and smooth.
4. **Start with short sessions.** If you're new to gargling, begin with short sessions of 15–30 seconds to allow your throat muscles to adjust to the sensation.
5. **Gradually increase duration.** As you become more comfortable, gradually increase the duration by 10–15 seconds until you can gargle for up to a minute.
6. **Focus on the vibrations.** Pay attention to the vibrations in your throat. They are key to engaging the vagus nerve and promoting a calming effect.
7. **Practice multiple times a day.** You can incorporate gargling into your daily routine—during your morning routine, after meals, or whenever you need a quick moment of relaxation.

Incorporating gargling into your daily routine helps stimulate the vagus nerve regularly, offering a simple yet effective way to support your emotional well-being.

### Singing

**Purpose:** Singing is another effective way to engage the vagus nerve. Whether in the shower or as part of your daily routine, singing helps regulate emotions and promote relaxation.

1. **Choose a song you enjoy.** Pick a song that feels uplifting or calming, whether it's a favorite tune or a simple melody.
2. **Find a comfortable space.** Sing where you feel comfortable, such as in the shower or in your car, where you can sing freely.
3. **Sing slowly and mindfully.** Focus on the act of singing, allowing yourself to fully experience the sound and vibration of your voice. Let the vibrations calm your body and mind.
4. **Immerse yourself in the moment.** Enjoy singing, relaxing, and letting go of any stress.
5. **Continue for a few minutes.** Sing for 3–5 minutes or longer if you have time.

*Incorporating Vocal Exercises Into Your Daily Routine*

**Purpose:** Integrating vocal exercises can easily become part of your everyday routine, whether through singing, humming, or chanting.

1. **Sing in the shower.** Let the acoustics and steam enhance your experience while enjoying the calming vibrations of your voice.
2. **Hum during your commute.** Turn your drive or commute into a moment of calm by humming to yourself, helping to reduce stress before or after work.
3. **Chant during meditation.** Incorporate chanting "OM" into your meditation practice to deepen your relaxation and enhance your mind-body connection.
4. **Repeat daily.** By adding these small moments to your day, you will notice a shift in positive emotional regulation and resilience over time.

The psychological benefits of vocal exercises are extensive. Regular practice can help reduce stress, enhance relaxation, and improve mood. Humming, chanting, or singing sends calming signals to your brain, reducing the production of stress hormones. This helps to create a sense of emotional stability, making it easier to handle daily challenges. Over time, you may notice that you feel more balanced, resilient, and capable of managing your emotions. Vocal exercises offer a simple yet powerful way to support your mental health, providing immediate relief and long-term benefits.

Consider the story of June, a young woman who struggled with chronic anxiety. Traditional therapies had only taken her so far. She began incorporating gargling into her morning routine and humming during her evening commute. Over time, she noticed a significant reduction in her anxiety levels. Her chest tightness eased, and she felt more grounded and present. For Carlos, a veteran dealing with PTSD, humming became a nightly ritual that helped him unwind and prepare for sleep. The vibrations calmed his racing mind and relieved the tension in his body. These real-life examples highlight the practical impact of these techniques, showing that even the simplest actions can lead to profound changes in emotional health.

## YOGA POSES ACTIVATE THE VAGUS NERVE

The benefits of yoga extend beyond physical flexibility. Specific yoga poses can stimulate the vagus nerve, helping to release stored tension and enhance the mind-body connection. For trauma survivors, this can mean a significant reduction in symptoms like anxiety and hypervigilance. The practice encourages a deeper awareness of bodily sensations, promoting long-term healing from trauma. By focusing on breath and movement, yoga helps regulate the nervous system, making it easier to manage stress and emotions. This holistic approach supports overall well-being, offering a pathway to recovery that integrates both mind and body.

These yoga poses are designed to gently activate the vagus nerve, promoting healing, emotional regulation, and a sense of calm. The focus is on mindful movement and deep, rhythmic breathing to engage the parasympathetic nervous system, helping you feel grounded and safe during your practice.

*Child's Pose (Balasana)*

**Purpose:** Child's Pose is a restorative position that encourages deep relaxation and activates the vagus nerve by promoting slow, deep breathing.

1. **Start on your knees.** Kneel on the floor with your big toes touching and knees slightly apart.
2. **Sit back on your heels.** Gently lower your hips to rest on your heels.
3. **Extend your arms forward.** Reach your arms forward on the mat and lower your torso, bringing your forehead to rest on the mat.
4. **Focus on your breath.** Take slow, deep breaths, feeling your abdomen expand against your thighs. Let the gentle compression of your body calm your nervous system.
5. **Hold for 5–10 breaths.** Stay in Child's Pose for several deep breaths, focusing on relaxation and releasing any tension in your body.

### Cat-Cow Pose (*Marjaryasana-Bitilasana*)

**Purpose:** Cat-Cow Pose gently stretches the spine and promotes rhythmic movement paired with breath, helping to stimulate the vagus nerve.

1. **Get on your hands and knees.** Start in a tabletop position with your wrists directly under your shoulders and knees under your hips.
2. **Inhale into Cow Pose.** As you inhale, arch your back, lift your chest, and gaze forward. Let your belly drop toward the mat.
3. **Exhale into Cat Pose.** As you exhale, round your spine, tuck your chin to your chest, and draw your belly toward your spine.
4. **Focus on the rhythm.** Repeat this flow, moving with the rhythm of your breath, inhaling into Cow Pose and exhaling into Cat Pose.
5. **Continue for 5–10 rounds.** Perform this movement for several rounds, allowing your breath to guide each transition.

### Bridge Pose (*Setu Bandhasana*)

**Purpose:** Bridge Pose strengthens the back and legs while gently stimulating the vagus nerve through mindful breathing and opening the chest.

1. **Lie on your back.** Start by lying on your back with your knees bent and feet flat on the floor, hip-width apart.
2. **Press through your feet.** Press your feet firmly into the ground and lift your hips toward the ceiling, keeping your shoulders grounded.

3. **Engage your core.** As you lift your hips, engage your core and glutes to support the pose. Keep your neck relaxed and chin slightly tucked.
4. **Breathe deeply.** Take deep, rhythmic breaths, expanding your chest with each inhale.
5. **Hold for 5–7 breaths.** Hold Bridge Pose for several breaths, then slowly lower your hips to the mat.

*Warrior I Pose (Virabhadrasana I)*

**Purpose:** Warrior I is a standing pose that builds strength, balance, and focus while encouraging deep breathing and body awareness to engage the vagus nerve.

1. **Stand with feet wide apart.** Stand tall with your feet wide apart, approximately three to four feet.
2. **Turn one foot outward.** Turn your right foot 90 degrees outward and angle your left foot slightly inward.
3. **Bend your front knee.** Bend your right knee, ensuring it is aligned over your ankle. Keep your left leg straight.
4. **Extend your arms.** Raise both arms overhead, reaching toward the ceiling with your palms facing each other.
5. **Breathe deeply.** Focus on taking deep, steady breaths as you hold the pose, feeling the strength in your body.
6. **Hold for 5–7 breaths.** Hold Warrior I for several breaths, switch sides, and repeat on the other leg.

These poses can be practiced individually or as part of a more extensive yoga flow. Focus on deep breathing and mindful movement in each pose to engage the vagus nerve and promote emotional regulation. Try humming while holding these poses for an added boost, as the vibration can further stimulate the vagus nerve and deepen your sense of calm. Incorporating these yoga poses and humming into your routine can help reduce stress, calm the nervous system, and support overall well-being.

## EXPLORING VAGUS NERVE STIMULATION (VNS) DEVICES

Vagus nerve stimulation (VNS) devices are designed to activate the vagus nerve, promoting relaxation, reducing stress, and enhancing overall nervous system balance. One popular option is the **Apollo Neuro**, a device that delivers gentle vibrations to the skin to influence the nervous system. However, several other VNS devices offer unique approaches to stimulating the vagus nerve:

- **Nurosym:** A noninvasive transcutaneous auricular vagus nerve stimulator (taVNS) that stimulates the nerve through the ear.
- **Pulsetto:** A wearable device that provides cervical vagus nerve stimulation via the neck, aimed at reducing stress and anxiety.
- **Hoolest:** A handheld device designed to stimulate the vagus nerve, potentially helping reduce anxiety and improve mood.
- **Truvaga Plus:** An updated version of the Truvaga 350, offering quick and gentle vagus nerve stimulation for stress relief.
- **Neuvana Xen:** Headphones that deliver electrical micropulses to the left ear, targeting the auricular branch of the vagus nerve.

- **gammaCore:** A handheld device approved for treating cluster headaches, offering noninvasive vagus nerve stimulation.

In addition to these devices, **transcutaneous electrical nerve stimulation (TENS)** units—commonly used for pain relief—can also be adapted for vagus nerve stimulation. This method, known as **transcutaneous auricular vagus nerve stimulation (taVNS)**, involves applying electrical impulses to specific areas of the ear, such as the tragus and cymba conchae, which are directly connected to the vagus nerve.

Standard TENS units can be equipped with specialized ear clip electrodes for this purpose. Studies suggest that taVNS may help reduce inflammation, alleviate symptoms of depression, and promote relaxation by activating the parasympathetic nervous system. However, proper use is essential. Consulting with a healthcare professional to ensure correct settings, placement, and technique is highly recommended before starting taVNS therapy.

When considering a VNS device, exploring the available options and tailoring your choice to your specific needs with guidance from a healthcare professional can help you maximize the benefits of this innovative approach to stress management and nervous system regulation.

# 6

# HEART RATE VARIABILITY BIOFEEDBACK FOR EMOTIONAL MASTERY

> *"Heart Rate Variability is the language of your nervous system, offering insight into your body's ability to adapt and thrive."*
>
> — UNKNOWN

Imagine sitting in a quiet room, feeling a sense of calm wash over you as you watch a small screen displaying the rhythmic beats of your heart. Each beat tells a story, reflecting your body's ability to handle stress and maintain balance. This is the essence of heart rate variability (HRV) biofeedback, a powerful tool for understanding and improving emotional resilience. By learning to monitor and regulate your HRV, you can gain insights into your body's stress responses and take proactive steps to enhance your well-being.

## HEART RATE VARIABILITY EXPLAINED

Heart rate variability (HRV) measures the variation in time between consecutive heartbeats, known as R-R intervals. Unlike a metronome's steady rhythm, a healthy heart exhibits slight fluctuations in beat-to-beat timing, reflecting a well-regulated nervous system. These variations indicate a balance between the sympathetic nervous system (fight or flight) and the parasympathetic nervous system (rest and digest). High HRV signifies adaptability—your body can efficiently shift between stress and relaxation, a hallmark of resilience and overall wellness.

Heart rate variability (HRV) does not have a one-size-fits-all "ideal" range because it varies from person to person based on factors like age, fitness, lifestyle, and overall health. However, there are general trends that can serve as helpful benchmarks. For young adults in their 20s and 30s, HRV is typically higher, often falling between 60–100 milliseconds (ms) or more. As people reach their 40s and 50s, HRV decreases slightly, usually ranging from 40–80 ms. By the time you are in your 60s and beyond, it is normal for HRV to decline further, commonly falling between 20–60 ms. While these ranges offer a general idea of what to expect, focusing on your personal baseline and patterns over time is more important than comparing yourself to a standard number.

A high HRV indicates your nervous system's flexibility, enabling quick recovery from stress and maintaining emotional balance. People with higher HRV often easily handle daily challenges, bouncing back quickly from difficult situations. In contrast, low HRV is associated with chronic stress, anxiety, and physical health issues such as cardiovascular disease. A consistently low HRV suggests the body remains in a heightened state of alertness, unable to fully relax and recover, which can lead to inflammation, high blood pressure, and mental health disorders.

HRV is a powerful tool for understanding both physical and emotional health. Monitoring HRV provides insights into how well your body manages and recovers from stress. For example, a declining HRV may signal prolonged stress or insufficient rest, while an improving HRV indicates successful recovery and resilience. By regularly tracking HRV, you can make informed decisions about your well-being and adopt practices that strengthen your nervous system and enhance your overall quality of life.

## HOW HRV REFLECTS TOTAL PHYSIOLOGICAL BALANCE

HRV is a comprehensive marker of your body's ability to regulate across multiple systems. It reflects the balance between the **sympathetic** and **parasympathetic nervous systems**, showcasing how efficiently your body can transition between stress and relaxation. A higher HRV signifies adaptability—

your heart, brain, and body work harmoniously to maintain homeostasis and effectively respond to life's challenges.

The cardiovascular system is central to HRV. When relaxed, your heart rate slows, and the intervals between beats vary more. During stress, your heart rate speeds up, and the intervals become more consistent. This variability indicates a healthy heart capable of adapting to changing conditions like a car smoothly shifting gears. A well-regulated cardiovascular system, reflected in higher HRV, supports physical performance, stress resilience, and overall heart health.

HRV is closely linked to **respiratory sinus arrhythmia (RSA)**—the natural variation in heart rate during the breathing cycle. When you inhale, your heart rate increases, and when you exhale, it decreases. This dynamic interplay between the heart and lungs is a critical component of HRV. Practicing deep, slow breathing enhances RSA, boosting HRV and promoting relaxation.

The **endocrine system** also influences HRV by releasing stress hormones like cortisol and adrenaline. Chronic stress and low HRV often go hand in hand, reflecting prolonged exposure to these hormones, which strains the body over time. By monitoring HRV, you can assess your body's response to stress and take proactive steps to reduce its impact, such as adopting relaxation techniques, mindfulness, or lifestyle changes.

Moreover, HRV reveals valuable insights into the immune system. Chronic stress and low HRV are linked to inflammation and weakened immune defenses. High HRV, on the other hand, reflects a balanced state where the body can effectively manage stress and maintain a robust immune response. Practices like mindfulness, regular exercise, and adequate rest can improve HRV, strengthening your immune system and overall health.

Finally, HRV connects to the **gut-brain axis** via the vagus nerve. This nerve plays a critical role in HRV and digestive health, promoting gut motility and reducing inflammation. Low HRV can indicate vagus nerve dysfunction, potentially leading to digestive issues. Enhancing vagal tone through HRV-improving techniques supports better digestion, gut health, and emotional well-being, demonstrating the interconnected nature of mind and body.

By understanding and improving HRV, you unlock a deeper awareness of your body's physiological regulation. It is not just a measure of heart health—it reflects your ability to adapt, recover, and thrive in a constantly changing world.

## UNLOCKING WELLNESS WITH HRV BIOFEEDBACK

Heart rate variability (HRV) biofeedback is a powerful tool for managing stress, enhancing emotional regulation, and building resilience. HRV biofeedback empowers you to make adjustments that promote calm and balance by providing real-time data on how your body responds to stress. As a biomarker for your nervous system, HRV offers a clear picture of your stress levels and adaptability. Low HRV often signals that your body struggles to manage stress, while higher HRV reflects resilience and flexibility—hallmarks of emotional and physical well-being.

One of the most transformative aspects of HRV biofeedback is its ability to make emotional improvements measurable. Often, progress in mental health can feel abstract and complex to track. HRV biofeedback changes that by showing tangible evidence of your efforts. For instance, practicing deep breathing or mindfulness exercises regularly can lead to an observable increase in your HRV over time. This confirmation validates your techniques and motivates you to stay consistent. Therapists can also use this data to tailor treatment plans, ensuring their interventions align with your unique needs.

In addition to tracking progress, HRV biofeedback is a powerful self-regulation tool. As you engage in relaxation techniques like diaphragmatic breathing or meditation, you can see immediate improvements in your HRV, indicating a shift toward a more balanced nervous system. This feedback loop reinforces the effectiveness of these practices, helping you refine them for a more significant impact. Over time, you gain greater control over your emotional responses, enabling you to recover more quickly from stress and maintain a stable, calm state, even in challenging situations.

HRV biofeedback is particularly effective in managing conditions like anxiety and depression, which often involve an overactivated sympathetic nervous system. Chronic fight-or-flight states can exhaust the body and mind, making it difficult to find relief. Practicing HRV biofeedback techniques can calm the nervous system, reduce anxiety, and improve your mood. Regular practice rebalances the nervous system, allowing smoother transitions between stress and relaxation, which is essential for maintaining emotional and physical health.

Beyond emotional regulation, HRV biofeedback enhances overall resilience. Training your nervous system to adapt flexibly helps you recover faster from life's challenges, whether work pressures, personal relationships, or unexpected events. This resilience reduces the risk of long-term stress-related health issues and equips you to face challenges with a balanced mind and body.

HRV biofeedback also promotes harmony between the parasympathetic (rest-and-digest) and sympathetic (fight-or-flight) systems, essential for optimal functioning. When these systems are balanced, you feel energized, calm, and focused. This balance supports mental health and boosts physical well-being, reducing inflammation, improving heart health, and strengthening the immune system.

By combining real-time insights with actionable techniques, HRV biofeedback empowers you to take control of your wellness. Whether used in therapy or as part of your daily routine, it offers a measurable and effective way to enhance emotional regulation, build resilience, and improve overall health and quality of life.

## A STEP-BY-STEP GUIDE TO IMPROVING HRV

Heart rate variability (HRV) biofeedback is an invaluable tool for understanding and improving your emotional resilience and stress management. To harness its benefits, it is essential to understand how HRV is measured and how biofeedback works. HRV monitoring devices use sensors, such as those in smartwatches, chest straps, or wearable rings, to detect the tiny variations between heartbeats, known as R-R intervals. These sensors track your heart's electrical activity, transmitting real-time data to an app or monitoring device. The result is a clear picture of your autonomic nervous system's balance, showing how well your body transitions between stress and relaxation.

Once the data is collected, the patterns in your HRV readings can be analyzed to assess your body's ability to manage stress. High HRV generally reflects a well-regulated nervous system, while low HRV suggests that your body is under stress or struggling to recover. By tracking trends, you can pinpoint how specific activities or events affect your nervous system. For example, you might notice a significant drop in HRV during a stressful meeting but see an improvement after practicing mindfulness or deep breathing. These insights allow you to identify what best regulates your nervous system.

HRV biofeedback goes beyond monitoring—it provides actionable techniques to improve your HRV in real time. Exercises like paced breathing are particularly effective. By following a pattern such as inhaling for four seconds, holding for four seconds, and exhaling for six seconds, you stimulate the vagus nerve and activate the parasympathetic nervous system. This calms your body, reduces stress, and increases HRV. Other interventions include mindfulness meditation, progressive muscle relaxation, and cold exposure, which train your body to respond to stress more adaptively.

Beyond biofeedback sessions, certain lifestyle practices can significantly improve HRV over time. Moderate physical activity, such as walking, swimming, or cycling, strengthens cardiovascular health and boosts HRV. Relaxation techniques like yoga or mindfulness meditation promote a balanced autonomic nervous system, making it easier for your body to recover from stress.

Additional interventions, like cold exposure and vocal exercises, can also enhance HRV. Taking cold showers, immersing your face in cold water, or humming, chanting, or singing stimulates the vagus nerve, promoting relaxation and boosting HRV. These simple, accessible practices make it easy to support your nervous system daily, enhancing stress management and emotional regulation.

By combining HRV biofeedback with lifestyle changes and targeted interventions, you can improve your body's adaptability, promote balance, and foster greater well-being. Whether through real-time feedback or regular habits, these strategies offer powerful tools to strengthen your resilience and emotional health.

## TOP TOOLS FOR TRACKING HRV

In today's world, technology has made monitoring your heart rate variability (HRV) easier than ever. Various wearable devices and mobile apps offer convenient ways to track HRV and gain insights into your body's stress levels and recovery. Wearable devices like the Apple Smart Watch, Oura Ring, Polar H10 chest strap, and Whoop Strap are popular for their accuracy and ease of use. These devices continuously monitor your heart rate and provide real-time feedback on your HRV. Mobile apps like Elite HRV and HeartMath offer detailed insights and guided exercises to help you improve your HRV, making integrating these practices into your daily routine easier.

When choosing an HRV monitoring device, consider your individual needs, accuracy requirements, and budget. If you're looking for a simple, user-friendly option, the Oura Ring might be a good fit. It offers comprehensive health tracking, including HRV, sleep, and activity levels. The Polar H10 chest strap provides high accuracy for those needing more detailed data. It is often used by athletes and researchers. Whoop Strap is another excellent choice, offering in-depth recovery and strain analysis. Selecting a device that aligns with your lifestyle and provides the level of detail you need to make informed decisions about your health is essential.

To ensure accurate and consistent HRV monitoring, follow a few essential tips. First, measure your HRV at the same time each day, preferably in the morning before you start your daily activities. This helps maintain consistency and provides a clear picture of your baseline HRV. Second, make sure your device is positioned correctly and calibrated. For example, if using a chest strap, ensure its snug and positioned correctly. Third, avoid consuming caffeine or strenuous activities before measuring your HRV, as these can temporarily affect your readings. Finally, use your HRV data to make informed decisions about your health practices, adjusting your routine to support better emotional and physical well-being.

### INTERPRETING HRV DATA FOR YOUR MENTAL HEALTH

Interpreting HRV data starts with understanding the metrics provided by your monitoring device. When you look at your HRV readings, you see a snapshot of your autonomic nervous system's balance. A high HRV is a sign that your body is managing stress well, while a low HRV indicates that your body may be struggling. For instance, if you notice a consistently low HRV, it suggests that your sympathetic nervous system is overactive, keeping you in a state of fight or flight. On the other hand, a high HRV suggests a well-regulated system where the parasympathetic branch is effectively helping you relax and recover.

Recognizing trends and patterns in your HRV data over time can provide valuable insights into your emotional and physical health. By tracking your HRV daily, you can identify what activities or events affect your stress levels. For example, you might see a dip in HRV on days with high work stress or poor sleep, indicating that these factors impact your nervous system. Conversely, you might notice an increase in HRV after practicing mindfulness or engaging in physical activity, showing that these practices are beneficial. Understanding these patterns helps you make informed decisions about your lifestyle and stress management strategies.

By consistently monitoring your HRV, you can set benchmarks and goals for improvement. If your HRV improves after certain activities, you can incorporate more of these into your routine. For example, suppose your HRV increases after a session of deep breathing. In that case, it indicates that this practice is effectively calming your nervous system. This real-time feedback empowers you to take control of your mental health, making adjustments as needed to enhance your well-being. HRV data serves as a guide, helping you navigate your journey toward better emotional resilience and stress management.

## POWERFUL TESTIMONIALS AND CASE STUDIES

Studies have consistently demonstrated the effectiveness of HRV biofeedback in improving emotional regulation and mental health. Research published by the National Institutes of Health highlights significant reductions in symptoms of anxiety and depression among participants who engaged in regular HRV biofeedback sessions. These findings underscore the value of HRV biofeedback as a reliable method for

managing stress and enhancing overall well-being. Another study conducted with older adults showed that HRV biofeedback training led to substantial improvements in emotional stability and resilience, even in those with limited social interactions.

Consider the case of David, a veteran who struggled with PTSD. His nights were filled with relentless nightmares and days with hypervigilance. Traditional therapies offered limited relief. When David began HRV biofeedback, he initially found it challenging to stay consistent. However, over time, he noticed subtle changes. His HRV readings improved, indicating better regulation of his nervous system. As he continued, his anxiety levels decreased, and he experienced fewer moments of hypervigilance. The real-time feedback provided a sense of control, empowering him to manage his symptoms more effectively.

Testimonials from individuals who have reduced their anxiety through HRV biofeedback are equally compelling. Susie, a mental health patient, shared how HRV biofeedback transformed her life. She had been battling anxiety for years, feeling constantly on edge. Through regular HRV biofeedback sessions, she learned to recognize patterns in her stress responses and apply techniques to calm her nervous system. "Seeing my HRV improve gave me hope," she said. "I felt like I had a tool to manage my anxiety, and it made a world of difference."

Mental health professionals also attest to the effectiveness of HRV biofeedback. Dr. Jones, a clinical psychologist, incorporates HRV biofeedback into his practice. "It is a game-changer," he explains. "Providing clients with real-time data on their stress levels allows for more personalized and effective treatment plans. The visual feedback helps clients understand their progress, which is incredibly motivating."

In this chapter, we have explored the importance of HRV biofeedback, practical techniques to improve HRV, and how to interpret your HRV data for better mental health. Understanding these concepts allows you to develop a more balanced and resilient nervous system, paving the way for improved emotional well-being and overall health.

# 7

# THE RHYTHM OF RESILIENCE WITH HRV EXERCISES

> "The rhythm of the heart is the rhythm of life. Tune into it, and you'll find your way back to balance."
>
> — UNKNOWN

Imagine a stressful day at work where your mind is racing, and tension builds. HRV biofeedback offers a way to regain control. By using a device or app, you can receive real-time feedback on your heart rate variability (HRV), helping you adjust your breathing and mindset to promote calm and emotional regulation. This practice enables you to manage stress, reduce anxiety, and build resilience over time.

Remember to grab your free bonus worksheets by SCANNING THE BARCODE BELOW! These tools are designed to enhance the exercises in this chapter and guide you on your healing journey.

## GETTING STARTED WITH HRV BIOFEEDBACK

HRV biofeedback is accessible and easy to incorporate into daily life. Devices like wearables or apps guide you through breathing exercises while providing immediate feedback. First, find a quiet space, attach the sensor, and follow the guided instructions. Techniques like resonant breathing—breathing at a steady rate of about five to seven breaths per minute—synchronize your heart rate with your breath, fostering deep relaxation and coherence. Visualization, such as imagining a serene beach or forest, enhances these effects, promoting emotional stability and stress reduction.

*Using HRV for Trauma Management*

HRV biofeedback is a compassionate tool for managing trauma symptoms, helping to identify and regulate physiological responses. Start by establishing a baseline HRV under relaxed conditions, which is a reference for monitoring stress triggers. Awareness of triggers—like specific thoughts or situations—enables you to apply immediate interventions such as diaphragmatic breathing or visualization to counteract stress responses.

Setting realistic goals, like reducing anxiety or improving calm, helps guide your practice and track progress. Real-time feedback from your device lets you see which techniques work best, refining your approach to managing trauma and building emotional resilience.

## BUILDING A CALMER MIND AND BODY

HRV biofeedback tools and apps make incorporating these practices into your routine more manageable. Breathing apps like iBreathe or Breathwrk provide guided exercises with visual or timed cues to help maintain an ideal rhythm for improving HRV. These tools ensure consistency and effectiveness, helping you regulate your nervous system and find calm in moments of stress.

By practicing HRV biofeedback regularly, you can create a feedback loop of growth and balance, leading to lasting improvements in emotional and physical well-being.

***Resonance Frequency Breathing***

**Purpose:** Resonance frequency breathing is a powerful technique that synchronizes your heart rate with your breath to optimize heart rate variability (HRV). You create a harmonious rhythm that activates the parasympathetic nervous system by breathing at a specific pace, typically five to seven breaths per minute. This practice reduces stress and anxiety, improves emotional regulation, promotes relaxation, and strengthens resilience to life's challenges. Physically, it enhances cardiovascular health and helps regulate the body's response to stress, making it an ideal exercise for mental and physical well-being.

1. **Find a comfortable position.** Sit or lie down comfortably with your back supported. Close your eyes and begin with a few deep, centering breaths to prepare yourself for the exercise.
2. **Set up your HRV device.** Attach your HRV sensor and start your monitoring device. Make sure it is tracking your heart rate variability so you can monitor changes throughout the exercise.
3. **Breathe at your resonant frequency.** Inhale deeply through your nose for a count of five. Hold your breath briefly, then exhale slowly through your mouth for a count of five. The goal is to achieve a breathing rate of five to seven breaths per minute. Continue this pattern, synchronizing your breath with your heart rate to optimize your HRV.

4. **Monitor HRV feedback.** Watch the feedback on your device and note how your HRV responds to this specific breathing rhythm. Aim for a steady, coherent heart rate pattern that reflects improved HRV.
5. **Practice for 10–20 minutes.** Continue resonance frequency breathing for 10 to 20 minutes. As your HRV improves, you should feel a deep sense of calm and emotional balance.

*Diaphragmatic Breathing*

**Purpose:** Diaphragmatic breathing, or deep belly breathing, is a simple yet highly effective technique that stimulates the parasympathetic nervous system, promoting a state of calm and relaxation. By breathing deeply into the diaphragm, you engage your body's natural "rest-and-digest" response, which helps reduce stress, lower heart rate, and enhance overall emotional stability. This technique eases anxiety and tension, improves lung function, lowers blood pressure, and supports a balanced nervous system. It is a powerful tool for both mental clarity and physical health.

1. **Sit or lie down comfortably.** Find a quiet space where you can sit with your back straight or lie down comfortably with your arms resting at your sides. Close your eyes and take a few slow breaths to center yourself.
2. **Start the HRV monitoring device.** Begin the HRV monitoring on your device or app to track your progress. Ensure the sensor is attached and calibrated correctly to monitor your heart rate variability.
3. **Breathe into your diaphragm.** Place one hand on your chest and the other on your abdomen. Inhale deeply through your nose, allowing your diaphragm to expand fully while keeping your chest still. Your abdomen should

rise with each breath. Hold your breath briefly, then slowly exhale through your mouth, feeling your abdomen fall. Focus on making each exhalation longer than your inhalation to engage the parasympathetic nervous system.
4. **Focus on HRV feedback.** As you breathe deeply, pay attention to the real-time HRV feedback from your device. Notice how your HRV improves as you relax into the breathing rhythm.
5. **Practice for 10–20 minutes.** Continue diaphragmatic breathing for 10 to 20 minutes, allowing your body to relax fully. Your HRV should stabilize and increase, signaling a shift into a more relaxed state.

*Guided Imagery*

**Purpose:** Guided imagery is a therapeutic technique that combines deep breathing with vivid mental visualization to promote emotional healing and optimize heart rate variability (HRV). By immersing yourself in a peaceful, imagined setting, such as a serene beach or a tranquil forest, you engage your senses and shift your mind from stress to relaxation. This practice enhances emotional resilience, reduces anxiety, and fosters physical healing by improving HRV. Guided imagery helps calm the nervous system, making it a valuable tool for emotional well-being and physical balance.

1. **Prepare your space.** Sit or lie down in a quiet, comfortable area. Close your eyes and take a few deep breaths, allowing your body to relax.
2. **Begin HRV monitoring.** Start your HRV device to track your heart rate variability during the guided imagery exercise.

3. **Visualize a calming scene.** As you breathe deeply, imagine yourself in a peaceful setting—a beach, a forest, or any place that brings you a sense of calm. Engage all your senses. Feel the warmth of the sun, hear the gentle waves, or smell the fresh air.
4. **Sync your breathing with the imagery.** Continue breathing deeply and slowly as you immerse yourself in the calming imagery. Imagine the air you breathe in is filled with peace, and with each exhalation, release tension and stress.
5. **Monitor HRV.** Watch your HRV feedback as you deepen your visualization and breathing. Notice how your heart rate variability improves as your mind and body relax into the imagery.
6. **Practice for 10–20 minutes.** Continue the guided imagery exercise for 10 to 20 minutes, letting yourself fully immerse in the scene and enjoying the calming effects on your HRV.

*Progressive Muscle Relaxation (PMR)*

**Purpose:** Progressive muscle relaxation (PMR) is an effective technique that involves tensing and relaxing each muscle group to reduce physical tension and stress. By consciously working through the body—from your toes to your head—you release muscle tightness and activate the parasympathetic nervous system, which promotes relaxation and improves heart rate variability (HRV). PMR is highly beneficial for managing anxiety, relieving stress, and promoting better sleep. Mentally, it helps increase awareness of where your body holds tension, empowering you to release it for greater physical and emotional balance.

1. **Find a relaxed position.** Sit or lie down in a quiet space. Make sure you are comfortable, with your arms at your sides and your eyes closed.
2. **Start HRV monitoring.** Turn on your HRV biofeedback device and ensure the sensor is attached correctly. This will allow you to track changes in your HRV as you release tension from your body.
3. **Tense and relax each muscle group.** Start with your toes. Tense the muscles for 5–10 seconds, then release, exhaling deeply as you relax the muscles completely. Work your way up through each muscle group—feet, calves, thighs, abdomen, chest, arms, shoulders, neck, and face—tensing and relaxing each group in turn.
4. **Pay attention to HRV feedback.** As you move through each muscle group, observe how tensing and relaxing affect your HRV. Notice the improvement in your heart rate variability as you release tension.
5. **Practice for 10–20 minutes.** Continue the exercise for 10 to 20 minutes, allowing your HRV to stabilize and increase as your body fully relaxes.

**What to Track**

1. **Daily HRV Scores**
   - Record your HRV measurements before and after each session of breathing or PMR exercises to see how your heart rate variability changes.

2. **Exercise Performed**
   - Note whether you practiced a breathing technique (such as resonant breathing or visualization) or progressive muscle relaxation (PMR).
3. **Duration of Practice**
   - Track how long you spent on each exercise—whether it was 10, 15, or 20 minutes.
4. **Combined Techniques**
   - If you combined deep breathing with PMR or visualization, indicate this on your worksheet. Combining techniques can amplify the benefits, so tracking these instances will be insightful.
5. **Outcome Notes**
   - Write down any noticeable physical or emotional changes after each session. This might include reduced stress, less muscle tension, improved mood, better focus, or greater emotional stability.
6. **Long-Term Trends**
   - Over time, compare your results to identify patterns. Which techniques led to the most significant improvements in your HRV? What exercises helped the most with reducing anxiety or promoting relaxation?

By consistently tracking these factors, you will better understand how each technique influences your mental and physical health. This data can also help you refine your practice to focus on the most effective methods for improving your HRV and managing stress.

## MAKING HRV BIOFEEDBACK PART OF YOUR ROUTINE

Incorporating HRV biofeedback can significantly improve your mental health and emotional resilience. Consistent practice stabilizes your emotional state and trains your nervous system to respond more flexibly to stress. Over time, this continuous engagement with HRV biofeedback helps you better cope with daily challenges, leading to greater emotional balance and a more fulfilling life.

Making HRV biofeedback a regular part of your routine does not have to be complicated. You can start with short sessions of HRV-focused breathing exercises in the morning to set a calm tone for the day or in the evening to wind down before bed. These brief moments of mindfulness can anchor you, making it easier to manage stress throughout the day. Additionally, quick HRV biofeedback exercises during work breaks can provide immediate relief, helping you regain focus and composure. Combining dedicated daily practice with on-the-go sessions ensures consistency and immediate stress management.

HRV biofeedback can be integrated with other wellness practices, such as somatic exercises and vagus nerve stimulation, to enhance its benefits. For example, you might begin with a body scan to identify areas of tension, follow it with deep breathing to activate the parasympathetic nervous system, and then use HRV biofeedback to monitor your progress. This holistic approach addresses the mind and body, fostering deeper relaxation and emotional regulation.

Lifestyle choices also play a vital role in improving HRV. A balanced diet rich in nutrients supports overall health and boosts HRV, with omega-3-rich foods like fish and flaxseeds being particularly beneficial. Regular physical activity, such as yoga, tai chi, or brisk walking, improves cardiovascular health and enhances HRV. Adequate sleep is another critical factor—poor sleep lowers HRV, making it harder to manage stress. Establishing a consistent sleep routine and creating a restful environment can significantly improve both sleep quality and HRV.

By making HRV biofeedback a consistent part of your routine and pairing it with healthy lifestyle habits, you can enhance your ability to manage stress, improve emotional resilience, and promote overall well-being.

## STUDIES ON HRV FOR ANXIETY AND TRAUMA

*Overcoming Anxiety Through HRV Biofeedback*

Linda, a young woman with generalized anxiety disorder, had tried various therapies and medications without much success. She decided to incorporate HRV biofeedback into her daily routine. Using a wearable device, Linda practiced deep breathing and progressive muscle relaxation. The real-time feedback from the device helped her understand how these techniques impacted her anxiety levels. Over time, Linda noticed a significant reduction in her symptoms. She felt more in control of her emotions. She was better equipped to handle stressful situations, demonstrating the power of HRV biofeedback in managing anxiety.

*Trauma Survivor Finding Calm*

Peter, a veteran dealing with trauma-related anxiety, incorporated HRV biofeedback into his recovery plan. Using a biofeedback device, he practiced visualization and resonant breathing daily. The visual feedback from the device showed him how these techniques improved his HRV, helping him manage his anxiety more effectively. Over time, Peter's anxiety attacks became less frequent, and he developed a greater sense of emotional balance, allowing him to reclaim control over his emotional well-being.

## Evidence-Based Studies Supporting HRV Biofeedback for Emotional Health

1. **Lehrer et al. (2020)** conducted a study showing that HRV biofeedback significantly reduces symptoms of anxiety and stress. The research demonstrated that individuals who practiced HRV biofeedback experienced improved autonomic nervous system regulation, reducing stress levels and enhancing emotional resilience.
2. **Gevirtz (2013)** found that HRV biofeedback helps individuals with trauma-related symptoms, particularly those with PTSD. The study indicated that HRV biofeedback can regulate the body's stress response, leading to improvements in anxiety management and emotional stability in trauma survivors.
3. **Schoenberg and David (2014)** reviewed multiple studies on HRV biofeedback and concluded that it is an effective tool for managing emotional disorders like generalized anxiety and depression. The studies revealed that HRV biofeedback increases parasympathetic nervous system activity, promoting relaxation and improving emotional regulation.

# 8

# BRINGING IT TOGETHER—NEUROSOMATIC THERAPY'S HEALING FORMULA

> "The integration of body and mind creates a powerful synergy, unlocking the true potential for growth and resilience."
>
> — BESSEL VAN DER KOLK

Picture this: A veteran named Steve, who has been grappling with PTSD, finds himself in a cycle of anxiety and hypervigilance. Traditional therapy has offered some respite, but his body still reacts as if it is in a war zone. One day, he is introduced to an integrative approach called NeuroSomatic Therapy, which is a therapy that combines somatic therapy, vagus nerve stimulation (VNS), and heart rate variability (HRV) biofeedback. Within weeks, Steve starts to notice significant changes. By tuning into his body's signals, using specific techniques to regulate his nervous system, and tracking his progress in real time, Steve begins to reclaim his life. This chapter explores how integrating these therapies can offer profound healing.

## HOW NEUROSOMATIC THERAPY IS HARMONY AT WORK

Integrating somatic therapy with VNS and HRV biofeedback enhances both physiological and psychological outcomes, creating a comprehensive, whole-body approach to mental health. This NeuroSomatic combination addresses emotional regulation, resilience, and stress relief more effectively than any therapy alone. You engage in a holistic healing process by focusing on the body's physical responses to trauma and stress and then applying techniques to calm the nervous system. These therapies can be easily practiced within a 30-minute daily routine, making them accessible even for busy individuals seeking mental health support.

The complementary nature of these therapies reinforces one another. Somatic therapy helps you recognize and release physical tension, VNS calms your nervous system, and HRV biofeedback provides real-time data to track your progress. The physiological harmony enhances the regulation of the autonomic nervous system, promoting emotional resilience. This integration not only improves emotional regulation but also significantly reduces symptoms of PTSD, anxiety, and depression. You can see how your body responds to different techniques, making adjustments as needed for optimal results.

The therapeutic outcomes of combining these modalities are profound. Faster recovery from trauma, reduced symptoms of anxiety and depression, and long-term mental health improvements are just a few benefits. Let us explain how to integrate these therapies into a manageable daily routine. For instance, you can start with a body scan combined with diaphragmatic breathing while monitoring your HRV. This helps you become aware of any tension in your body and use your breath to release it. Grounding techniques followed by humming or chanting can further enhance this effect, helping you assess HRV trends and make necessary adjustments.

Incorporating vagus nerve exercises during somatic experiencing sessions while tracking HRV can offer additional benefits. For example, practicing gentle movements or stretches while focusing on your breath can activate the vagus nerve, promoting relaxation. Using feedback from HRV biofeedback, you can see how these exercises impact your nervous system, allowing you to refine your techniques. Integrating somatic techniques into daily VNS routines provides a holistic approach to well-being, making it easier to manage stress and maintain emotional balance.

Consider the real-life case of Janet, a trauma survivor who benefited immensely from this integrated approach. By incorporating NeuroSomatic Therapy into her daily routine, Janet was able to manage her symptoms more effectively. She found stability through body scans and breathing exercises, monitored her progress with HRV biofeedback, and used VNS to calm her nervous system. Similarly, Nick, a veteran recovering from PTSD, experienced significant improvements through the NeuroSomatic combined techniques. By integrating these therapies into his daily routine, Nick reduced his hypervigilance and anxiety, finding a sense of peace that had long eluded him.

Practitioners specializing in trauma recovery have also noted the practical benefits of this combined approach. Mental health professionals emphasize that integrating these therapies enhances clinical outcomes by providing a comprehensive treatment plan. For instance, Dr. Emily Johnson, a psychologist, highlights how these techniques have helped her clients achieve better emotional regulation and reduced symptoms of PTSD. The real-time feedback from HRV biofeedback allows for personalized adjustments, making the therapy more effective.

By creating a structured yet flexible routine incorporating these techniques, you can take significant strides toward improved mental and physical health. This integrative approach offers a powerful toolset for managing stress, enhancing resilience, and promoting overall well-being.

Remember to grab your free bonus worksheets by SCANNING THE BARCODE BELOW! These tools are designed to enhance the exercises in this chapter and guide you on your healing journey.

## EXERCISES FOR ANXIETY, STRESS, AND TRAUMA

This subchapter focuses on practical, step-by-step NeuroSomatic exercises that can be completed in less than 30 minutes a day to help manage anxiety, stress, trauma, and physical health challenges. Each exercise combines proven techniques like deep breathing, grounding, vagus nerve stimulation, and HRV biofeedback to create a quick and effective daily routine. Designed for ease of use, these exercises empower you to take control of your emotional and physical well-being, providing immediate relief while building long-term resilience.

*Grounding With Diaphragmatic Breathing*

**Purpose:** This exercise provides immediate relief from anxiety and stress by grounding you in the present moment and calming your nervous system through deep breathing and physical connection.

1. **Get comfortable.** Sit or stand in a comfortable position where you can focus.
2. **For the 5-4-3-2-1 grounding technique**, identify:
   - Five things you can see.
   - Four things you can touch.
   - Three things you can hear.
   - Two things you can smell.
   - One thing you can taste.

3. **Incorporate deep breathing.** Practice slow belly breathing throughout, focusing on expanding your abdomen as you inhale and relaxing it as you exhale.
4. **Add vagus nerve stimulation.** On each exhale, hum gently to activate your vagus nerve and deepen relaxation.
5. **Use biofeedback.** Monitor your HRV with a biofeedback device, adjusting your breathing to maintain a steady, calm rhythm.
6. **Repeat as needed.** Perform this exercise until you feel calmer and more relaxed.

*Progressive Muscle Relaxation (PMR) With Resonant Frequency Breathing*

**Purpose:** This exercise helps release physical tension and promotes emotional calm by combining muscle relaxation with rhythmic breathing, effectively managing anxiety and reducing stress.

1. **Find a quiet space.** Sit or lie down in a quiet, comfortable spot.
2. **Tense and relax muscles.** Start with your feet, tensing each muscle group for a few seconds, then relax. Move upward through your body, ending with your face and head.
3. **Practice resonant breathing.** Inhale for five counts, hold briefly, and exhale for five counts.
4. **Monitor your HRV.** Use a biofeedback device to track the reduction in anxiety levels and fine-tune your breathing.
5. **Repeat as needed.** Perform this exercise until you feel calmer and more relaxed.

## Body Scan With Vagus Nerve Stimulation

**Purpose:** This exercise fosters deep relaxation and reduces stress by combining body awareness with vagus nerve stimulation, helping to alleviate anxious sensations and promote emotional balance.

1. **Lie or sit comfortably.** Choose a position that allows you to focus on your body.
2. **Begin a body scan.** Slowly shift your attention to each part of your body, starting from your head and moving to your toes.
3. **Breathe deeply.** Maintain deep belly breathing throughout the exercise.
4. **Add vocalization.** Use gentle humming or chanting to stimulate the vagus nerve and enhance relaxation.
5. **Track your HRV.** Monitor your HRV to observe stress reduction and track progress over time.
6. **Repeat as needed.** Perform this exercise until you feel calmer and more relaxed.

## Alternate Nostril Breathing With Sensory Grounding

**Purpose:** This exercise helps calm the mind and reduce anxiety by combining breath regulation with sensory grounding, providing a comprehensive approach to managing stress and enhancing focus.

1. **Sit comfortably.** Hold a textured object in one hand for sensory grounding.

2. **Practice alternate nostril breathing.**
   - Close one nostril with your finger and inhale through the open nostril.
   - Switch nostrils and exhale through the opposite nostril.
3. **Combine breathing with touch.** Focus on the object's texture as you breathe to further distract from anxious thoughts.
4. **Monitor your HRV.** Use a biofeedback device to track the calming effects of the exercise.
5. **Repeat until calm.** Continue until you feel grounded and relaxed.

*Walking Grounding With Vagus Nerve Activation*

**Purpose:** This exercise combines mindful movement, breath focus, and vagus nerve stimulation to reduce anxiety, enhance emotional regulation, and ground you in the present moment.

1. **Walk slowly and mindfully.** Focus on each step as you move.
2. **Incorporate deep breathing.** Practice slow belly breathing as you walk.
3. **Add gentle humming.** Hum softly with each exhale to stimulate your vagus nerve.
4. **Use biofeedback.** Track your HRV to monitor emotional regulation in real time.
5. **Stay present.** Focus on the sensation of walking and breathing to ground yourself in the moment.
6. **Repeat until calm.** Continue until you feel grounded and relaxed.

## Deep Belly Breathing With Physical Grounding

**Purpose:** This exercise quickly alleviates stress and anxiety by anchoring you through physical grounding while calming your nervous system with deep, steady breathing.

1. **Find a grounded position.** Stand barefoot on the ground or sit with your feet flat on the floor to feel connected to the earth.
2. **Start deep belly breathing.** Inhale deeply through your nose, expanding your belly as you breathe in. Exhale slowly through your mouth, allowing your belly to relax.
3. **Focus on physical sensations.** Pay attention to the feeling of your feet connecting with the ground or the chair beneath you. Notice any sensations of stability and anchoring in your body.
4. **Use biofeedback.** Monitor your HRV with a biofeedback device to track your stress response. Adjust your breathing to maintain a calm, steady rhythm, aiming for smoother HRV patterns.
5. **Repeat and anchor the calm.** Continue the exercise until you notice a sense of calm and reduced stress. Practice regularly to strengthen your ability to ground yourself and manage stress effectively.

## Cold Exposure With Somatic Awareness

**Purpose:** This exercise helps manage stress and hypervigilance by using cold exposure to stimulate the vagus nerve, paired with somatic awareness and controlled breathing to promote calmness and emotional resilience.

1. **Prepare for cold exposure.** Take a cold shower or immerse your face in cold water.
2. **Focus on sensations.** Pay attention to how the cold feels on your skin.
3. **Maintain controlled breathing.** Practice deep, steady breaths to stay calm.
4. **Monitor HRV.** Track your HRV to observe how cold exposure affects your stress levels.
5. **Repeat regularly.** This technique builds resilience and reduces stress over time.

*Resonant Breathing With Body Scan*

**Purpose:** This exercise reduces stress and enhances relaxation by combining rhythmic breathing with a focused body scan, promoting greater body awareness and emotional balance.

1. **Find a comfortable position.** Sit or lie down where you can focus.
2. **Begin resonant breathing.** Inhale for five counts, hold briefly, and exhale for five counts.
3. **Perform a body scan.** Focus on each body part from head to toe, aligning the scan with your breath.
4. **Track your HRV.** Use biofeedback to ensure a balanced, calming breath pattern.
5. **Relax and reflect.** Note how this combination promotes relaxation and body awareness.

*Tai Chi Movements With Diaphragmatic Breathing and Humming*

**Purpose:** This exercise improves flexibility, balance, and emotional regulation by integrating mindful movement, deep breathing, and vagus nerve stimulation to reduce anxiety and promote relaxation.

1. **Practice slow tai chi movements.** Focus on flowing, mindful movements.
2. **Add deep breathing.** Coordinate each movement with deep diaphragmatic breathing.
3. **Incorporate humming.** Between movements, hum softly to activate the vagus nerve.
4. **Monitor your HRV.** Use biofeedback to observe stress reduction and adjust your technique as needed.
5. **Repeat for relaxation.** Continue until you feel calm and grounded.

## NEUROSOMATIC THERAPY A NEW ERA IN TRAUMA CARE

Trauma-informed care is a framework that prioritizes safety, trustworthiness, and empowerment for those who have experienced trauma. It acknowledges the widespread impact of trauma and understands potential paths for recovery. The core principles involve creating a safe environment, building trust, and empowering individuals by giving them control over their healing process. Trauma-informed care fosters a compassionate and supportive atmosphere, which is essential for those working through trauma, anxiety, and depression.

Combining NeuroSomatic Therapy within the trauma-informed care framework can significantly enhance the healing process. These techniques offer sensitive and supportive care by addressing both the physical and emotional aspects of trauma. For example, somatic therapy helps individuals recognize their body and its responses. At the same time, vagus nerve exercises promote relaxation and stability. HRV biofeedback provides real-time data, allowing individuals to monitor their progress and adjust as needed. This combined approach enhances safety and stabilization and promotes body awareness and self-regulation.

Consider the case of Melissa, a trauma survivor who found stability through this integrated approach. Melissa had been struggling with anxiety and hypervigilance, symptoms that traditional therapy alone could not fully address. Melissa learned to tune into her body's signals by incorporating somatic techniques. She practiced grounding exercises to stay present and used HRV biofeedback to monitor her stress levels. Vagus nerve exercises, like deep breathing and humming, helped her calm her nervous system. Over time, Melissa experienced significant improvements in her emotional regulation and overall well-being. Similarly, Francisco, a veteran with PTSD, benefited from trauma-informed somatic therapy combined with HRV biofeedback. By tracking his progress and using targeted exercises, Francisco managed to reduce his hypervigilance and anxiety, finding a sense of peace.

## Grounding With Diaphragmatic Breathing and HRV Biofeedback

**Purpose:** This exercise helps reduce hypervigilance, manage stress, and promote relaxation by combining grounding techniques, deep breathing, and real-time biofeedback.

1. **Find a grounded position.** Stand barefoot on the ground or hold a comforting object in your hands to create a sense of stability and connection.
2. **Begin deep belly breathing.** Inhale deeply through your nose, expanding your abdomen as you breathe in. Exhale slowly through your mouth, allowing your belly to relax fully.
3. **Incorporate humming.** As you exhale, hum softly to stimulate the vagus nerve and enhance relaxation.
4. **Use HRV biofeedback.** Monitor your HRV using a biofeedback device to track your stress levels in real time. Adjust your breathing rhythm to maintain a calm and steady pattern, focusing on smoother HRV readings.
5. **Repeat and anchor calmness.** Continue this exercise until you feel a reduction in hypervigilance and stress. Practice regularly to manage stress, promote physical recovery, and improve resilience to trauma.

## Body Scan With Resonant Breathing and Vagus Nerve Stimulation (VNS)

**Purpose:** This exercise helps manage PTSD symptoms by reducing physical tension and promoting relaxation through focused body awareness, resonant breathing, and vagus nerve stimulation.

1. **Find a comfortable position.** Sit or lie down in a quiet, comfortable space to focus on your body.
2. **Begin resonant breathing.** Inhale deeply through your nose for a count of five, hold briefly, then exhale slowly through your mouth for a count of five. Maintain a steady rhythm to encourage relaxation.
3. **Perform a body scan.** Gradually shift your focus to different parts of your body, starting from your head and moving downward. Pay special attention to areas of tension, such as your shoulders, jaw, or chest, and consciously release that tension as you breathe.
4. **Incorporate vocal humming.** As you exhale during the body scan, hum softly to stimulate the vagus nerve and deepen relaxation.
5. **Use HRV biofeedback.** Monitor your HRV with a biofeedback device to observe how your relaxation levels improve as you progress through the exercise. Adjust your breathing if needed to maintain a calm, steady rhythm.
6. **Conclude with reflection.** After completing the body scan, take a moment to notice how your body feels,

particularly in areas where tension has been released. Practice this technique regularly to enhance emotional regulation and overall well-being.

### Tai Chi Movements With Coherent Breathing and Vagus Nerve Stimulation

**Purpose:** This exercise helps reduce anxiety, manage hyperarousal, and improve flexibility and balance by combining mindful movement, coherent breathing, and vagus nerve stimulation.

1. **Prepare for tai chi practice.** Find a quiet space with enough room to move comfortably. Stand with your feet shoulder-width apart and your body relaxed.
2. **Practice slow, mindful movements.** Perform gentle tai chi movements, focusing on smooth, flowing motions. Keep your movements slow and deliberate.
3. **Incorporate coherent breathing.** Coordinate your movements with deep, rhythmic breathing. Inhale for a count of four as you begin a movement, and exhale for a count of four as you complete it.
4. **Add vocal humming.** Between movements, hum softly during your exhale to stimulate the vagus nerve and enhance relaxation.
5. **Use HRV biofeedback.** Track your HRV with a biofeedback device as you move and breathe. Adjust your technique as needed to maintain a calm, balanced state.
6. **Focus on balance and flexibility.** Pay attention to your body's alignment and muscles' feelings during each

motion. Allow the exercise to improve your balance and range of motion over time.

7. **Repeat for relaxation and centering.** Continue practicing for 10–15 minutes until you feel calmer and more centered. Use this exercise regularly to manage anxiety and hyperarousal effectively.

*Cold Exposure With Grounding and Diaphragmatic Breathing*

**Purpose:** This exercise helps manage hypervigilance, reduce inflammation, and improve mental and physical recovery by combining cold exposure, grounding techniques, diaphragmatic breathing, and vagus nerve stimulation.

1. **Prepare for cold exposure.** Choose a method of cold exposure, such as a cold shower or immersing your face in cold water.
2. **Engage in physical grounding.** Stand barefoot on the ground or hold a textured object to anchor yourself physically and mentally.
3. **Begin diaphragmatic breathing.** Inhale deeply through your nose, expanding your belly as you breathe in. Exhale slowly through your mouth, focusing on steady, controlled breathing.
4. **Incorporate vocal humming.** During each exhale, hum softly to stimulate the vagus nerve and enhance relaxation.
5. **Use HRV biofeedback.** Monitor your HRV with a biofeedback device to track your body's response to cold

exposure. Adjust your breathing to maintain a calm, balanced state.
6. **Focus on sensations.** Pay attention to the sensations of the cold on your skin and how your body responds. Use this awareness to stay grounded in the present moment.
7. **Conclude and reflect.** End the cold exposure session after 1–3 minutes or when you feel ready. Take a moment to notice the changes in your stress levels and how your body feels.
8. **Repeat this exercise.** Repeat regularly to build resilience and enhance your overall mental and physical health.

*Progressive Muscle Relaxation (PMR) With Guided Imagery and Vagus Nerve Stimulation*

**Purpose:** This exercise helps reduce muscle tension, enhance emotional stability, and manage PTSD symptoms by combining PMR, guided imagery, and vagus nerve stimulation.

1. **Find a comfortable position.** Sit or lie down in a quiet, comfortable space where you can focus without distractions.
2. **Begin progressive muscle relaxation (PM).** Start with your feet, tensing each muscle group for a few seconds before slowly releasing the tension. Gradually move upward through your body, focusing on one muscle group at a time, ending with your shoulders and jaw.
3. **Incorporate guided imagery.** As you relax each muscle group, visualize a safe, calming place like a beach, forest, or cozy room. Engage your senses by imagining this safe space's sights, sounds, and feelings.
4. **Add vocal humming.** During each exhale, hum softly to stimulate the vagus nerve and deepen relaxation.

5. **Use HRV biofeedback (optional).** Monitor your HRV with a biofeedback device to observe the calming effects and adjust your breathing for optimal relaxation.
6. **Complete the session.** Once you have relaxed all muscle groups, spend a moment fully immersed in your safe space visualization. Reflect on the calmness and sense of stability you have achieved.
7. **Repeat regularly.** Practice this exercise daily or whenever you experience heightened stress or PTSD symptoms to promote relaxation and emotional stability.

## CRAFTING A DAILY ROUTINE FOR BALANCE AND WELL-BEING

A structured daily routine can set a positive tone for your day, reduce stress, and enhance emotional resilience. Whether starting your morning, resetting midday, or winding down in the evening, intentional routines help you align with your goals and foster a sense of purpose.

*Morning Routine: Start Your Day Right*

Beginning your day with balance establishes clarity and emotional stability. Dedicating 30 minutes each morning to practices like cold water splashes, gentle stretches, deep breathing, and mindfulness journaling can energize your body and mind. Incorporate activities like vagus nerve stimulation exercises to enhance relaxation and emotional regulation. Research underscores the benefits of morning routines, showing they reduce stress, boost mental health, and promote a sense of purpose. Consistency is key—set a wake-up time, prepare the night before, and prioritize these activities as essential parts of your day.

*Midday Reset: Recharge and Refocus*

Taking short breaks during the day is essential for maintaining calm and focus. A 15–30-minute midday reset might include grounding exercises, HRV biofeedback, hydration, and guided meditation. These activities refresh your body and mind, improving productivity and reducing stress. Studies show regular breaks enhance well-being, prevent burnout, and improve job satisfaction. Use reminders, apps, or a designated quiet space to seamlessly integrate a midday reset into your routine.

*Evening Wind-Down: Prepare for Restful Sleep*

An evening wind-down helps your body transition into relaxation and prepares you for restorative sleep. Spend 30 minutes engaging in calming activities like gentle yoga, body scanning, gratitude journaling, and deep breathing exercises. These practices improve sleep quality and reduce stress. To make  this routine effective, establish a consistent bedtime, minimize screen time, and create a calming sleep environment with dim lighting and relaxing scents.

### *Customizing Your Routine*

Tailor your daily routine to suit your preferences and needs. Adjust the duration and intensity of activities to fit your schedule, and select techniques you enjoy, such as outdoor walks, creative journaling, or specific mindfulness practices. Personalized routines are more sustainable and engaging, enhancing their effectiveness.

### *Tracking Progress With Daily Logs*

Tracking your activities and symptoms through daily logs can provide valuable insights into your healing journey. Use the downloadable worksheets included in this book to monitor mood, symptoms, and progress. These templates simplify the tracking process, allowing you to identify patterns, celebrate successes, and refine your practices. Regularly reviewing your logs helps you make informed adjustments to your routine, ensuring continuous progress toward your goals.

Committing to a personalized, consistent routine and leveraging the tools provided can create a foundation for long-term emotional and physical well-being.

## SETTING FUTURE GOALS FOR A PATH TO HEALING

Setting future goals is like planting seeds in a garden—they provide direction, motivation, and a sense of purpose as you work toward personal growth and healing. Goals help you focus on what matters most, keep you engaged during challenges, and allow you to measure progress and celebrate achievements. Both short- and long-term goals are essential: short-term goals offer immediate rewards and keep you motivated, while long-term goals help you envision the future and stay committed.

Begin by crafting SMART goals—Specific, Measurable, Achievable, Relevant, and Time-bound. For instance, instead of saying, "I want to feel less stressed," a SMART goal might be, "I will practice deep breathing for 10 minutes each morning for the next two weeks." Breaking larger aspirations into manageable steps makes progress feel attainable and actionable.

Identify areas for growth, such as improving emotional regulation, reducing stress, or enhancing physical health. For example, if your goal is to establish a mindfulness practice, start with short-term steps like learning a technique, dedicating five minutes daily to practice, and reflecting weekly on your progress.

Leverage your strengths and resources to make these goals realistic and empowering. Reflect on your skills and the support systems available to you. Build on what you already have to create an achievable and motivating plan. Regularly review and adjust your goals to align with your evolving needs. Setting aside time each month to evaluate your progress can keep you focused and flexible.

Creative goals that resonate with your healing journey can be especially rewarding. You might aim to establish a mindfulness routine, learn a new skill like painting, or contribute to a mental health advocacy project. These goals provide a sense of accomplishment and reinforce your commitment to healing.

Maintaining motivation can be challenging but is essential for success. Break goals into smaller tasks, celebrate victories along the way, and surround yourself with supportive individuals who encourage and hold you accountable. Visual reminders like a vision board or journal can help keep your goals at the forefront of your mind. If motivation wanes, revisit your initial reasons for setting the goal and adjust as needed to match your current priorities.

Find ways to make the process enjoyable and sustainable. Join a supportive community, track your progress with an app, or integrate your goals into activities you already enjoy. Remember, each step forward—no matter how small—is progress worth celebrating. By staying committed and adaptable, you can achieve your goals and continue to grow and heal.

### OVERCOMING SETBACKS AND SUSTAINING PROGRESS

Setbacks and plateaus are a normal part of the healing journey and do not signify failure. Progress is rarely linear, often marked by ups and downs. Acknowledging this reality can help reduce frustration and self-doubt, allowing you to stay committed to your goals. By understanding that setbacks are a natural part of growth, you can approach them with patience and resilience.

When setbacks arise, identify potential triggers and adjust your approach. If a technique like deep breathing no longer feels effective, try alternatives such as progressive muscle relaxation or HRV biofeedback. Seeking support from a therapist or a support group can offer fresh perspectives and encouragement. Re-evaluating your goals may also help you refocus and stay on track. Small, consistent efforts are often the most impactful, so embrace a long-term perspective and keep moving forward.

Real-life stories can provide inspiration. Rachel, for instance, faced a setback when her anxiety resurfaced after months of progress. Instead of giving up, she adjusted her routine to include grounding exercises and sought additional support, regaining control over her symptoms. Similarly, Mark broke through a plateau in his PTSD recovery by incorporating new techniques like cold exposure and HRV biofeedback. Their perseverance illustrates how adaptability and persistence can lead to breakthroughs.

Maintaining motivation is critical for sustained progress. Setting new goals, celebrating milestones, and finding inspiration from success stories can keep you engaged. An accountability partner, support group, or regular check-ins with a therapist can provide ongoing encouragement. When motivation wanes, revisit your initial reasons for starting this journey, reflect on your aspirations, and consider trying new techniques to keep things fresh and exciting.

Balancing self-care with daily responsibilities is a challenge for many. Competing demands from work, family, and personal life often make it hard to prioritize self-care. Effective time management, such as creating a structured daily schedule or using time blocking, can help you integrate self-care practices into your routine. Short, efficient activities like mindful eating or quick stretches can make self-care more manageable, while apps for guided meditation offer added support.

Setting boundaries is essential for protecting your self-care time. Communicate your needs and avoid unnecessary commitments to ensure self-care remains a priority. Integrating self-care into existing routines, like practicing mindfulness during meals or breaks, can make these practices feel less burdensome and more sustainable.

Addressing skepticism or doubt is another common hurdle, especially if previous therapies have not worked. Building trust in new techniques can be achieved by starting small with manageable exercises and gradually tracking your progress. Evidence-based research and testimonials from others can also reinforce confidence in these methods. Seeking professional guidance ensures you are on the right path, while an open-minded and flexible approach can lead to unexpected positive outcomes.

Embracing challenges, staying motivated, and prioritizing self-care create a strong foundation for growth and healing. With persistence and adaptability, you will continue progressing, even in the face of obstacles.

**Share the Power of Somatic Therapy**

Healing is a continuous process, and every step forward is a step toward a brighter future. This is your opportunity to make that future more accessible to other people too. All you have to do is leave a short review.

Simply by sharing your honest opinion of this book and a little about how it's helped you, you'll show new readers where they can find the guidance they need to benefit from somatic therapy themselves.

## IN UNDER 1 MINUTE
### YOU CAN HELP OTHERS JUST LIKE YOU BY LEAVING A REVIEW!

★ ★ ★ ★ ★

Thank you so much for your support. I wish you every success as you move forward with your healing journey.

**Scan the QR code below**

# CONCLUSION

> "Healing doesn't mean the damage never existed. It means the damage no longer controls your life."
>
> — UNKNOWN

As we reach the end of this journey together, let us take a moment to revisit the core insights we have explored. Throughout this book, we delved into NeuroSomatic Therapy, which integrates somatic therapy, vagus nerve stimulation, and heart rate variability (HRV) biofeedback. These approaches offer a comprehensive method to heal trauma, anxiety, and depression. We have seen how scientific evidence supports these techniques and how they can be practically applied to foster long-term emotional and physical well-being.

Our journey began with understanding the intricate mind-body connection. We explored how trauma and stress impact the central and autonomic nervous systems and how targeted interventions can restore balance. We discussed the role of the vagus nerve and the benefits of monitoring HRV to gauge and enhance our stress responses. Through real-life examples and guided exercises, we saw how these techniques can be woven into daily routines, offering tangible relief and improvement.

The vision and purpose of this book have been clear from the start. My goal is to provide you, whether you are a mental health practitioner or someone struggling with mental health symptoms, with a step-by-step guide to these integrative therapeutic techniques. This book aims to empower you with the knowledge and tools necessary for a holistic approach to healing. By combining somatic therapy with vagus nerve exercises and HRV biofeedback, we can achieve profound and lasting changes in mental health.

Key takeaways from our exploration include the importance of body awareness, the power of the vagus nerve in regulating emotions, and the effectiveness of HRV biofeedback in managing stress. We have learned actionable strategies, such as grounding exercises, deep breathing techniques, and mindful movement, all designed to bring balance and calm to the nervous system. These techniques are not just theoretical but practical tools you can use daily.

Healing is not a destination but a continuous journey. I encourage you to keep practicing the techniques you have learned here. Consistency and perseverance are crucial. Healing takes time, and it is essential to be patient with yourself. Continue to learn and adapt these practices to fit your evolving needs. Remember, every small step forward is progress.

For mental health practitioners, I urge you to integrate these methods into your practice and tailor them to meet each client's unique needs. Share your success stories and feedback to contribute to the growing body of evidence supporting these integrative approaches. Your role is vital in helping your clients navigate their healing journeys.

To all my readers, you have the power to take control of your healing journey. You have the tools and knowledge to improve your mental health significantly. Believe in your ability to heal and grow. This book is not just a guide but a companion on your path to resilience and well-being.

I have included appendices with additional readings, websites, and support groups for further resources and support. These resources can provide ongoing assistance and deepen your understanding of the techniques discussed in this book. Professional organizations and online communities are valuable places to connect with others on similar journeys.

I want to express my deepest gratitude to the experts, therapists, and researchers whose work has made this book possible. Thank you to my readers for your trust and dedication to your healing journey. Your commitment to improving your mental health is inspiring.

As we conclude, I want to leave you with an uplifting message. Healing is a challenging path, but it is also a journey of empowerment and resilience. Each step you take brings you closer to a better quality of life. Embrace the process and know that you have the strength to overcome any obstacle. The healing journey is about overcoming pain and finding joy, peace, and fulfillment.

You have taken the first step by exploring this book. Now, continue to walk the path with courage and hope. Remember, you are not alone. There is a community of support and resources available to you. Together, we can achieve a brighter, healthier future.

# RESOURCES

## WEARABLE DEVICES FOR HEART RATE AND HEALTH TRACKING

- **Apple Smart Watch**
    - Use: Tracks heart rate, HRV, activity, and stress levels to support overall wellness.
    - Where to Get: Available at Apple stores or online.
    - More Info: https://www.apple.com/watch.
- **Oura Ring**
    - Use: Monitors HRV, sleep patterns, and recovery to optimize health and stress management.
    - Where to Get: Purchase online at Oura's website.
    - More Info: https://ouraring.com.
- **Polar H10 Chest Strap**
    - Use: A highly accurate heart rate monitor for HRV and fitness tracking during exercise.
    - Where to Get: Available online or at fitness retailers.
    - More Info: https://www.polar.com.
- **Whoop Strap**
    - Use: Monitors HRV, sleep, strain, and recovery to help optimize performance and wellness.
    - Where to Get: Subscription-based purchase online at Whoop's website.
    - More Info: https://www.whoop.com.

## MOBILE APPS FOR HRV, BREATHING, AND STRESS MANAGEMENT

- **Elite HRV**
    - Use: Measures HRV and provides insights into stress and recovery.
    - Where to Get: Available on iOS and Android app stores.
    - More Info: https://elitehrv.com.
- **HeartMath**
    - Use: Offers biofeedback for stress reduction and emotional regulation through HRV tracking.
    - Where to Get: Download from app stores or purchase paired devices on their website.
    - More Info: https://www.heartmath.com.
- **iBreathe**
    - Use: Guides breathing exercises for relaxation and anxiety management.
    - Where to Get: Free on iOS and Android app stores.
    - More Info: https://ibreatheapp.com.
- **Breathwrk**
    - Use: Provides guided breathing exercises to reduce stress, improve focus, and enhance relaxation.
    - Where to Get: Available on iOS and Android app stores.
    - More Info: https://www.breathwrk.com.
- **Calm**
    - Use: Combines guided meditations, sleep stories, and relaxation techniques to reduce stress and anxiety.
    - Where to Get: Available on iOS and Android app stores.
    - More Info: https://www.calm.com.

- **Insight Timer**
  - Use: Features a library of meditations, including breathing and mindfulness exercises, tailored to your needs.
  - Where to Get: Free on iOS and Android app stores.
  - More Info: https://www.insighttimer.com.

## WEARABLE DEVICES FOR NERVOUS SYSTEM REGULATION

- **Apollo Neuro**
  - Use: Delivers gentle vibrations to the skin to reduce stress and improve focus.
  - Where to Get: Order from Apollo Neuro's website.
  - More Info: https://apolloneuro.com
- **Sensate**
  - Use: A wearable device that uses low-frequency sound vibrations to calm the nervous system and enhance relaxation.
  - Where to Get: Purchase online at Sensate's website.
  - More Info: https://www.getsensate.com

## VAGUS NERVE STIMULATION DEVICES

- **Nurosym**
  - Use: Noninvasive device that stimulates the vagus nerve through the ear for relaxation and stress relief.
  - Where to Get: Purchase online at Nurosym's website.
  - More Info: https://nurosym.com.
- **Pulsetto**
  - Use: Wearable device providing cervical vagus nerve stimulation via the neck to reduce stress and anxiety.

- Where to Get: Order online at Pulsetto's website.
- More Info: https://pulsetto.com.
- **Hoolest**
  - Use: Handheld device stimulating the vagus nerve to reduce anxiety and improve mood.
  - Where to Get: Available online at Hoolest's website.
  - More Info: https://hoolest.com.
- **Truvaga Plus**
  - Use: Offers quick, gentle vagus nerve stimulation for stress relief.
  - Where to Get: Purchase online at Truvaga's website.
  - More Info: https://truvaga.com.
- **Neuvana Xen**
  - Use: Headphones that deliver electrical micro-pulses to the left ear, targeting vagus nerve stimulation.
  - Where to Get: Purchase on Neuvana's website.
  - More Info: https://neuvanalife.com.
- **gammaCore**
  - Use: Handheld device approved for treating cluster headaches through noninvasive vagus nerve stimulation.
  - Where to Get: Available with a prescription or online.
  - More Info: https://www.gammacore.com.

## TENS UNITS FOR VAGUS NERVE STIMULATION

- **TENS Units for taVNS**
  - Use: Adapted TENS units with ear clip electrodes for transcutaneous auricular vagus nerve stimulation (taVNS) to promote relaxation, reduce inflammation, and alleviate depression symptoms.

- Where to Get: Purchase TENS units and specialized electrodes online or at medical retailers.
- More Info: https://www.ncbi.nlm.nih.gov/pmc/articles/PMC5534856/.

## ADDITIONAL TOOLS FOR STRESS MANAGEMENT AND WELLNESS

- **Muse Meditation Headband**
  - Use: Provides real-time biofeedback during meditation to track and enhance relaxation.
  - Where to Get: Purchase online at Muse's website.
  - More Info: https://choosemuse.com.
- **Somavedic Devices**
  - Use: Creates a field that mitigates EMF exposure and promotes physical and mental harmony.
  - Where to Get: Available online at Somavedic's website.
  - More Info: https://somavedic.com.
- **Blue Light Blocking Glasses**
  - Use: Reduces exposure to blue light, improving sleep quality and reducing eye strain.
  - Where to Get: Available at various online and retail stores.
  - More Info: https://www.blublox.com.

## ONLINE RESOURCES

- *30 Grounding Techniques to Quiet Distressing Thoughts*
  https://www.healthline.com/health/grounding-techniques
- *7 Wearable Biofeedback Devices For HRV & Stress Training*
  https://www.diygenius.com/hrv-biofeedback-training/

- *Autonomic Nervous System: Anatomy, Function, Disorders* https://www.verywellmind.com/what-is-the-autonomic-nervous-system-2794823
- *Biofeedback-Assisted Resilience Training for Traumatic ...* https://www.ncbi.nlm.nih.gov/pmc/articles/PMC6754694/
- *Body Scan Meditation: Benefits and How to Do It* https://www.healthline.com/health/body-scan-meditation
- *Clinical perspectives on vagus nerve stimulation* https://www.ncbi.nlm.nih.gov/pmc/articles/PMC9093220/
- *Effect of Resonance Breathing on Heart Rate Variability ...* https://www.ncbi.nlm.nih.gov/pmc/articles/PMC8924557/
- *Exercise is an all-natural treatment to fight depression* https://www.health.harvard.edu/mind-and-mood/exercise-is-an-all-natural-treatment-to-fight-depression
- *Heart Rate Variability (HRV) Biofeedback for Anxiety* https://www.psychologytoday.com/us/blog/integrative-mental-health-care/201810/heart-rate-variability-hrv-biofeedback-anxiety
- *Heart Rate Variability (HRV): What It Is and How You Can ...* https://my.clevelandclinic.org/health/symptoms/21773-heart-rate-variability-hrv
- *Heart rate variability as a biomarker for autonomic nervous ...* https://www.ncbi.nlm.nih.gov/pmc/articles/PMC3684221/
- *How Does Vagus Nerve Stimulation Reduce PTSD ...* https://www.psychologytoday.com/us/blog/the-athletes-way/202201/how-does-vagus-nerve-stimulation-reduce-ptsd-symptoms
- *Jumping into the Ice Bath Trend! Mental Health Benefits of ...* https://longevity.stanford.edu/lifestyle/2024/05/22/

jumping-into-the-ice-bath-trend-mental-health-benefits-of-cold-water-immersion/
- *Leveraging Neuroplasticity to Enhance Adaptive Learning* https://www.ncbi.nlm.nih.gov/pmc/articles/PMC6380941/
- *Long-term benefits of heart rate variability biofeedback ...* https://www.ncbi.nlm.nih.gov/pmc/articles/PMC9637191/
- *Non-Invasive Vagal Nerve Stimulation Effects on ... - NCBI* https://www.ncbi.nlm.nih.gov/pmc/articles/PMC5534856/
- *Nutrition and mental health: A review of current knowledge ...* https://www.ncbi.nlm.nih.gov/pmc/articles/PMC9441951/
- *Personalized Trauma Recovery Coaching for a Healing ...* https://traumarecoverysupport.com/individualized-trauma-healing/
- *Post-traumatic stress disorder: the neurobiological impact ...* https://www.ncbi.nlm.nih.gov/pmc/articles/PMC3182008/
- *Somatic experiencing – effectiveness and key factors of a ...* https://www.ncbi.nlm.nih.gov/pmc/articles/PMC8276649/
- *Somatic Experiencing for Posttraumatic Stress Disorder* https://www.ncbi.nlm.nih.gov/pmc/articles/PMC5518443/
- *Somatic Experiencing in CBT: Enhancing Trauma Treatment* https://bayareacbtcenter.com/the-role-of-somatic-experiencing-in-cbt/
- *Somatic Experiencing: Supporting Trauma Resolution and ...* https://traumahealing.org/
- *Somatic Psychology: Meaning and Origins* https://meridianuniversity.edu/content/somatic-psychology-meaning-and-origins

- *Somatic Therapy vs Somatic Experiencing: Understanding ...* https://aurainstitute.org/somatics-training-4/2024/06/10/somatic-therapy-vs-somatic-experiencing-understanding-the-key-differences
- *The brain-body disconnect: A somatic sensory basis for ...* https://www.ncbi.nlm.nih.gov/pmc/articles/PMC9720153/
- *The effect of heart rate variability biofeedback training on ...* https://pubmed.ncbi.nlm.nih.gov/28478782/
- *The effects of music relaxation and muscle ...* https://www.ncbi.nlm.nih.gov/pmc/articles/PMC4253375/
- *The Mental Health Benefits of Deep Breathing* https://diversushealth.org/mental-health-blog/the-mental-health-benefits-of-deep-breathing/
- *The polyvagal theory: New insights into adaptive reactions ...* https://www.ncbi.nlm.nih.gov/pmc/articles/PMC3108032/
- *The role of early Reichian theory in the development ...* https://www.researchgate.net/publication/232505604_The_role_of_early_Reichian_theory_in_the_development_of_Gestalt_therapy
- *Transcutaneous vagal nerve stimulation blocks stress ...* https://www.ncbi.nlm.nih.gov/pmc/articles/PMC8474180/
- *Trauma-Informed Yoga: How it Heals, Benefits, and Poses ...* https://psychcentral.com/health/what-is-trauma-informed-yoga
- *Vagus Nerve Stimulation for Posttraumatic Stress Disorder* https://www.health.mil/Reference-Center/Publications/2021/04/26/PHCoE-Evidence-Brief-Vagus-Nerve-Stimulation-for-Posttraumatic-Stress-Disorder-508
- *Vagus nerve stimulation: Benefits, risks, and more* https://www.medicalnewstoday.com/articles/vagus-nerve-stimulation

**Detailed Resources in Alphabetical Order**

- Blanaru, M., Bloch, B., Vadas, L., Arnon, Z., Ziv, N., Kremer, I., & Haimov, I. (2012). The effects of music relaxation and muscle relaxation techniques on sleep quality and emotional measures among individuals with posttraumatic stress disorder. *Mental Illness*, 4(2), e13. https://doi.org/10.4081/mi.2012.e13
- *Body scan meditation: Benefits and how to do it.* (2020, March 26). Healthline. https://www.healthline.com/health/body-scan-meditation
- Bremner, J. D., Gurel, N. Z., Jiao, Y., Wittbrodt, M. T., Levantsevych, O. M., Huang, M., Jung, H., Shandhi, M. H., Beckwith, J., Herring, I., Rapaport, M. H., Murrah, N., Driggers, E., Ko, Y.-A., Alkhalaf, M. L., Soudan, M., Song, J., Ku, B. S., Shallenberger, L., … Pearce, B. D. (2020). Transcutaneous vagal nerve stimulation blocks stress-induced activation of Interleukin-6 and interferon-γ in posttraumatic stress disorder: A double-blind, randomized, sham-controlled trial. *Brain, Behavior, & Immunity - Health*, 9, 100138. https://doi.org/10.1016/j.bbih.2020.100138
- Brom, D., Stokar, Y., Lawi, C., Nuriel-Porat, V., Ziv, Y., Lerner, K., & Ross, G. (2017a). Somatic experiencing for posttraumatic stress disorder: A randomized controlled outcome study. *Journal of Traumatic Stress*, 30(3), 304. https://doi.org/10.1002/jts.22189
- Brom, D., Stokar, Y., Lawi, C., Nuriel-Porat, V., Ziv, Y., Lerner, K., & Ross, G. (2017b). Somatic experiencing for posttraumatic stress disorder: A randomized controlled outcome study. *Journal of Traumatic Stress*, 30(3), 304. https://doi.org/10.1002/jts.22189

- Center, B. A. C. (2024, July 26). Somatic experiencing in CBT: Enhancing trauma treatment. *Bay Area CBT Center*. https://bayareacbtcenter.com/the-role-of-somatic-experiencing-in-cbt/
- Chaitanya, S., Datta, A., Bhandari, B., & Sharma, V. K. (2022). Effect of resonance breathing on heart rate variability and cognitive functions in young adults: A randomised controlled study. *Cureus, 14*(2), e22187. https://doi.org/10.7759/cureus.22187
- Evans, S., Seidman, L. C., Tsao, J. C., Lung, K. C., Zeltzer, L. K., & Naliboff, B. D. (2013). Heart rate variability as a biomarker for autonomic nervous system response differences between children with chronic pain and healthy control children. *Journal of Pain Research, 6*, 449. https://doi.org/10.2147/JPR.S43849
- *Exercise is an all-natural treatment to fight depression.* (2013, July 17). Harvard Health. https://www.health.harvard.edu/mind-and-mood/exercise-is-an-all-natural-treatment-to-fight-depression
- Goessl, V. C., Curtiss, J. E., & Hofmann, S. G. (2017). The effect of heart rate variability biofeedback training on stress and anxiety: A meta-analysis. *Psychological Medicine, 47*(15), 2578–2586. https://doi.org/10.1017/S0033291717001003
- Goggins, E., Mitani, S., & Tanaka, S. (2022a). Clinical perspectives on vagus nerve stimulation: Present and future. *Clinical Science (London, England: 1979), 136*(9), 695. https://doi.org/10.1042/CS20210507
- Goggins, E., Mitani, S., & Tanaka, S. (2022b). Clinical perspectives on vagus nerve stimulation: Present and future. *Clinical Science (London, England: 1979), 136*(9), 695. https://doi.org/10.1042/CS20210507

- Grajek, M., Krupa-Kotara, K., Białek-Dratwa, A., Sobczyk, K., Grot, M., Kowalski, O., & Staśkiewicz, W. (2022). Nutrition and mental health: A review of current knowledge about the impact of diet on mental health. *Frontiers in Nutrition, 9,* 943998. https://doi.org/10.3389/fnut.2022.943998
- *Grounding techniques: Exercises for anxiety, PTSD, and more.* (2019, May 24). Healthline. https://www.healthline.com/health/grounding-techniques
- *Heart rate variability (Hrv) biofeedback for anxiety.* (n.d.). Psychology Today. https://www.psychologytoday.com/us/blog/integrative-mental-health-care/201810/heart-rate-variability-hrv-biofeedback-anxiety
- *Heart rate variability (Hrv): What it is and how you can track it.* (n.d.). Cleveland Clinic. https://my.clevelandclinic.org/health/symptoms/21773-heart-rate-variability-hrv
- *Home.* (2024, September 30). Somatic Experiencing® International. https://traumahealing.org/
- *How does vagus nerve stimulation reduce PTSD symptoms?* (n.d.). Psychology Today. https://www.psychologytoday.com/us/blog/the-athletes-way/202201/how-does-vagus-nerve-stimulation-reduce-ptsd-symptoms
- *How the autonomic nervous system regulates body functions.* (n.d.). Verywell Mind. https://www.verywellmind.com/what-is-the-autonomic-nervous-system-2794823
- *Individualized trauma healing.* (n.d.). Trauma Recovery Support. https://traumarecoverysupport.com/individualized-trauma-healing/
- Kearney, B. E., & Lanius, R. A. (2022). The brain-body disconnect: A somatic sensory basis for trauma-related disorders. *Frontiers in Neuroscience, 16,* 1015749. https://doi.org/10.3389/fnins.2022.1015749

- Kizakevich, P. N., Eckhoff, R. P., Lewis, G. F., Davila, M. I., Hourani, L. L., Watkins, R., Weimer, B., Wills, T., Morgan, J. K., Morgan, T., Meleth, S., Lewis, A., Krzyzanowski, M. C., Ramirez, D., Boyce, M., Litavecz, S. D., Lane, M. E., & Strange, L. B. (2019). Biofeedback-assisted resilience training for traumatic and operational stress: Preliminary analysis of a self-delivered digital health methodology. *JMIR mHealth and uHealth*, *7*(9), e12590. https://doi.org/10.2196/12590
- Kuhfuß, M., Maldei, T., Hetmanek, A., & Baumann, N. (2021). Somatic experiencing – effectiveness and key factors of a body-oriented trauma therapy: A scoping literature review. *European Journal of Psychotraumatology*, *12*(1), 1929023. https://doi.org/10.1080/20008198.2021.1929023
- Lamb, D. G., Porges, E. C., Lewis, G. F., & Williamson, J. B. (2017). Non-invasive vagal nerve stimulation effects on hyperarousal and autonomic state in patients with posttraumatic stress disorder and history of mild traumatic brain injury: Preliminary evidence. *Frontiers in Medicine*, *4*, 124. https://doi.org/10.3389/fmed.2017.00124
- Pearce, A. K. (2022, January 16). 7 wearable biofeedback devices for HRV & stress training. *DIY Genius*. https://www.diygenius.com/hrv-biofeedback-training/
- Porges, S. W. (2009). The polyvagal theory: New insights into adaptive reactions of the autonomic nervous system. *Cleveland Clinic Journal of Medicine*, *76*(Suppl 2), S86. https://doi.org/10.3949/ccjm.76.s2.17
- Sherin, J. E., & Nemeroff, C. B. (2011). Post-traumatic stress disorder: The neurobiological impact of psychological trauma. *Dialogues in Clinical Neuroscience*, *13*(3), 263. https://doi.org/10.31887/DCNS.2011.13.2/jsherin

- Shetty, M. (2024, May 22). Jumping into the ice bath trend! Mental health benefits of cold water immersion | cognitive enhancement. *Lifestyle Medicine*. https://longevity.stanford.edu/lifestyle/2024/05/22/jumping-into-the-ice-bath-trend-mental-health-benefits-of-cold-water-immersion/
- Smith, E. W. (1975, October). *Https://www.researchgate.net/publication/232505604_The_role_of_early_Reichian_theory_in_the_development_of_Gestalt_therapy*. Researchgate.Net.
- *Somatic psychology: Meaning and origins*. (n.d.). Meridian University. https://meridianuniversity.edu/content/somatic-psychology-meaning-and-origins
- *Somatic therapy vs somatic experiencing: Understanding the key differences*. (n.d.). Aura Institute - Integrative Trauma & Somatic Therapy Training. https://aurainstitute.org/somatics-training-4/2024/06/10/somatic-therapy-vs-somatic-experiencing-understanding-the-key-differences
- Souza, P. M. de, Souza, M. de C., Diniz, L. A., Araújo, C. R. V., Lopez, M., Volchan, E., Orlando Fernandes, J., Sanchez, T. A., & Souza, G. G. L. (2022). Long-term benefits of heart rate variability biofeedback training in older adults with different levels of social interaction: A pilot study. *Scientific Reports*, *12*, 18795. https://doi.org/10.1038/s41598-022-22303-z
- The mental health benefits of deep breathing. (n.d.). *Diversus Health*. https://diversushealth.org/mental-health-blog/the-mental-health-benefits-of-deep-breathing/
- *Trauma-informed yoga: How it heals, benefits, and poses to try*. (2022, January 4). Psych Central. https://psychcentral.com/health/what-is-trauma-informed-yoga
- *Vagus Nerve Stimulation for Posttraumatic Stress Disorder*. (2021, March). Defense Health Agency. https://www.

health.mil/Reference-Center/Publications/2021/ 04/26/PHCoE-Evidence-Brief-Vagus-Nerve-Stimulation- for-Posttraumatic-Stress-Disorder-508
- *Vagus nerve stimulation: Benefits, risks, and more.* (2021, October 14). Medical News Today. https://www.medicalnewstoday.com/articles/vagus-nerve-stimulation
- Wilkinson, S. T., Holtzheimer, P. E., Gao, S., Kirwin, D. S., & Price, R. B. (2018). Leveraging neuroplasticity to enhance adaptive learning: The potential for synergistic somatic-behavioral treatment combinations to improve clinical outcomes in depression. *Biological Psychiatry, 85*(6), 454. https://doi.org/10.1016/j.biopsych.2018.09.004

# REFERENCES

## STUDIES ON THE IMPACT OF MIND-BODY THERAPIES

Aguilar-Raab, C., Stoffel, M., Hernández, C., Rahn, S., Moessner, M., Steinhilber, B., & Ditzen, B. (2021). Effects of a mindfulness-based intervention on mindfulness, stress, salivary alpha-amylase and cortisol in everyday life. *Psychophysiology, 58*(12), e13937. https://doi.org/10.1111/psyp.13937

Hayes, J. P., VanElzakker, M. B., & Shin, L. M. (2012). Emotion and cognition interactions in PTSD: A review of neurocognitive and neuroimaging studies. *Frontiers in Integrative Neuroscience, 6*. https://doi.org/10.3389/fnint.2012.00089

Jones, R. (2012). Oligodendrocyte transporters feed axons. *Nature Reviews Neuroscience, 13*(9), 601–601. https://doi.org/10.1038/nrn3316

Mehling, W. E., Wrubel, J., Daubenmier, J. J., Price, C. J., Kerr, C. E., Silow, T., Gopisetty, V., & Stewart, A. L. (2011). Body Awareness: A phenomenological inquiry into the common ground of mind-body therapies. *Philosophy, Ethics, and Humanities in Medicine, 6*(1), 6. https://doi.org/10.1186/1747-5341-6-6

Pariante, C. M., & Lightman, S. L. (2008). The HPA axis in major depression: Classical theories and new developments. *Trends in Neurosciences, 31*(9), 464–468. https://doi.org/10.1016/j.tins.2008.06.006

Stephen, A. (2016, August 17). Mindfulness practice leads to increases in regional brain grey matter density. *The Science of Meditation and Mindfulness.* https://thescienceofmeditation.org/2016/08/17/mindfulness-practice-leads-to-increases-in-regional-brain-grey-matter-density/

Tsai, J., Rosenheck, R. A., Decker, S. E., Desai, R. A., & Harpaz-Rotem, I. (2012). Trauma experience among homeless female veterans: Correlates and impact on housing, clinical, and psychosocial outcomes. *Journal of Traumatic Stress, 25*(6), 624–632. https://doi.org/10.1002/jts.21750

## SOMATIC THERAPY'S EFFECTIVENESS IN REDUCING PSTD ANXIETY AND DEPRESSION SYMPTOMS

Bartel, A., Jordan, J., Correll, D., Devane, A., & Samuelson, K. W. (2020). Somatic burden and perceived cognitive problems in trauma-exposed adults with post-traumatic stress symptoms or pain. *Journal of Clinical Psychology, 76*(1), 146–160. https://doi.org/10.1002/jclp.22855

Baten, E., & Desoete, A. (2018). Mathematical (Dis)abilities within the opportunity-propensity model: The choice of math test matters. *Frontiers in Psychology, 9*, 667. https://doi.org/10.3389/fpsyg.2018.00667

Tsai, J., Rosenheck, R. A., Decker, S. E., Desai, R. A., & Harpaz-Rotem, I. (2012). Trauma experience among homeless female veterans: Correlates and impact on housing, clinical, and psychosocial outcomes. *Journal of Traumatic Stress, 25*(6), 624–632. https://doi.org/10.1002/jts.21750

## SOMATIC THERAPY COMPARED TO TRADITIONAL TALK THERAPY

Chowdhury, I. A. (2023, February 27). *Depression: The Biochemical factors associated with development and progression of MDD - Specialized Therapy.* https://www.specializedtherapy.com/depression-2/, https://www.specializedtherapy.com/depression-2/

Kearney, B. E., & Lanius, R. A. (2022). The brain-body disconnect: A somatic sensory basis for trauma-related disorders. *Frontiers in Neuroscience, 16*, 1015749. https://doi.org/10.3389/fnins.2022.1015749

Young, C. (2006). One hundred and fifty years on: The history, significance and scope of body psychotherapy today. *Body, Movement and Dance in Psychotherapy, 1*(1), 17–28. https://doi.org/10.1080/17432970500468299

## VAGUS NERVE STIMULATION TO IMPROVE SYMPTOMS OF MENTAL HEALTH

Aaronson, S. T., Sears, P., Ruvuna, F., Bunker, M., Conway, C. R., Dougherty, D. D., Reimherr, F. W., Schwartz, T. L., & Zajecka, J. M. (2017). A 5-year observational study of patients with treatment-resistant depression treated with vagus nerve stimulation or treatment as usual: Comparison of response, remission, and suicidality. *The American Journal of Psychiatry, 174*(7), 640–648. https://doi.org/10.1176/appi.ajp.2017.16010034

Aguglia, A., Salvi, V., Maina, G., Rossetto, I., & Aguglia, E. (2011). Fibromyalgia syndrome and depressive symptoms: Comorbidity and clinical correlates. *Journal of Affective Disorders, 128*(3), 262–266. https://doi.org/10.1016/j.jad.2010.07.004

Breit, S., Kupferberg, A., Rogler, G., & Hasler, G. (2018). Vagus nerve as modulator of the brain–gut axis in psychiatric and inflammatory disorders. *Frontiers in Psychiatry, 9*, 44. https://doi.org/10.3389/fpsyt.2018.00044

Bremner, J. D. (2023). Vagal nerve stimulation for patients with stress-related psychiatric disorders and addictions. *Journal of Health Service Psychology, 49*(3), 129–135. https://doi.org/10.1007/s42843-023-00089-6

Chen, L. H., Heng Mak, T. S., Fan, Y., Yin Ho, D. T., Sham, P. C., Chu, L. W., & Song, Y.-Q. (2020). Associations between CLU polymorphisms and memory performance: The role of serum lipids in Alzheimer's disease. *Journal of Psychiatric Research, 129*, 281–288. https://doi.org/10.1016/j.jpsychires.2020.07.015

*Gammacore®, the first non-invasive vagus nerve stimulator applied at the neck, now available for adult patients in the u. S.* (n.d.). electroCore. https://www.electrocore.com/news/gammacore-the-first-non-invasive-vagus-nerve-stimulator-applied-at-the-neck-now-available-for-adult-patients-in-the-u-s/

Jerath, R., Edry, J. W., Barnes, V. A., & Jerath, V. (2006). Physiology of long pranayamic breathing: Neural respiratory elements may provide a mechanism that explains how slow deep breathing shifts the autonomic nervous system. *Medical Hypotheses, 67*(3), 566–571. https://doi.org/10.1016/j.mehy.2006.02.042

*Vagus nerve stimulator & reset vibrating wristband.* (n.d.). Apollo Neuro. https://apolloneuro.com/products/apollo-wearable

Ventriglio, A., Gentile, A., Stella, E., & Bellomo, A. (2015). Metabolic issues in patients affected by schizophrenia: Clinical characteristics and medical management. *Frontiers in Neuroscience, 9*. https://doi.org/10.3389/fnins.2015.00297

## IMPACT OF HRV BIOFEEDBACK TO MANAGE MENTAL HEALTH

Chen, L. H., Heng Mak, T. S., Fan, Y., Yin Ho, D. T., Sham, P. C., Chu, L. W., & Song, Y.-Q. (2020). Associations between CLU polymorphisms and memory performance: The role of serum lipids in Alzheimer's disease. *Journal of Psychiatric Research, 129*, 281–288. https://doi.org/10.1016/j.jpsychires.2020.07.015

Erratum. (2010). *Journal of Psychosomatic Research, 69*(5), 523. https://doi.org/10.1016/j.jpsychores.2010.07.001

Lehrer, P. M., & Gevirtz, R. (2014). Heart rate variability biofeedback: How and why does it work? *Frontiers in Psychology, 5*. https://doi.org/10.3389/fpsyg.2014.

00756

Schoenberg, P. L. A., & David, A. S. (2014). Biofeedback for psychiatric disorders: A systematic review. *Applied Psychophysiology and Biofeedback, 39*(2), 109–135. https://doi.org/10.1007/s10484-014-9246-9

Sim, Y.-S. (2022). Building coherence and increasing emotion regulation flexibility towards resilience: An experimental study in Singapore. In T. Hunt & L. M. Tan (Eds.), *Applied Psychology Readings* (pp. 10–42). Springer Nature Singapore. https://doi.org/10.1007/978-981-19-5086-5_2

Steffen, P. R., Bartlett, D., Channell, R. M., Jackman, K., Cressman, M., Bills, J., & Pescatello, M. (2021). Integrating breathing techniques into psychotherapy to improve HRV: Which approach is best? *Frontiers in Psychology, 12*, 624254. https://doi.org/10.3389/fpsyg.2021.624254

Xuan, L., Hua, S., Lin, L., & Jianli, Y. (2023). Gender differences in the predictive effect of depression and aggression on suicide risk among first-year college students. *Journal of Affective Disorders, 327*, 1–6. https://doi.org/10.1016/j.jad.2023.01.123

## IMPACT OF THE POWER OF ROUTINE ON MENTAL HEALTH

*Give me a break.* (n.d.). Https://Www.Apa.Org. https://www.apa.org/monitor/2019/01/break

*Leveling up: Supporting employees' psychological well-being for maximum return.* (n.d.). Https://Www.Apa.Org. https://www.apa.org/topics/healthy-workplaces/supporting-employee-psychological-well-being

Wu, C., Lu, J., Lu, S., Huang, M., & Xu, Y. (2020). Increased ratio of mature BDNF to precursor-BDNF in patients with major depressive disorder with severe anhedonia. *Journal of Psychiatric Research, 126*, 92–97. https://doi.org/10.1016/j.jpsychires.2020.05.010